Throughout 1985 the American Congress was considering major revisions of U.S. food and farm laws. The results of this process will affect food consumers and farmers in the U.S.A. and around the world. *Dirt Rich, Dirt Poor* is designed as a major reference point for the political discussions arising out of this legislation. It covers production, distribution and consumption of food, analyzes international as well as domestic problems, and presents new pathways out of the confusion.

Emphasizing public policy and programs, the book has chapters on: agricultural production; environmental and resource problems; food marketing; domestic hunger and nutrition; and world hunger and development. Each chapter discusses current problems and issues, describes past and existing policies in the area, and offers suggestions for new policy and programmatic approaches. A concluding chapter analyzes Congress's 1985 food and farm legislation and the political process that led to it.

Dirt Rich, Dirt Poor sets out broad goals for the food system, with an emphasis on equity for producers and consumers, security of the food supply, and resource and environmental protection.

THE AUTHORS

Joseph N. Belden is a Washington-based writer and attorney specializing in poverty, rural development, agriculture and food issues. He has worked for the U.S. Department of Agriculture and several other government agencies and private groups. He is at present working as a research specialist for the Housing Assistance Council in Washington.

And Vincent P. Wilber, Enid Kassner, Rus Sykes, Ed Cooney, Lynn Parker, Alan Sanders, Cynthia Schneider, Marsha Simon.

DIRT RICH, DIRT POOR

Alternative Policies for America

Already published in the series

DIRT RICH, DIRT POOR

AMERICA'S FOOD AND FARM CRISIS

Joseph N. Belden
and
Vincent P. Wilber
Enid Kassner
Rus Sykes
Ed Cooney
Lynn Parker
Alan Sanders
Cynthia Schneider
Marsha Simon

The Institute for Policy Studies / World Hunger Year

Routledge & Kegan Paul
New York and London

The Institute for Policy Studies, 1901 Que Street N.W., Washington, D.C., 20009, U.S.A., founded in 1963, is a transnational center for research, education, and social invention. IPS sponsors critical study of U.S. policy, and proposes alternative strategies and visions. Programs focus on national security, foreign policy, human rights, the international economic order, domestic affairs, and knowledge and politics.

First published in 1986
by Routledge & Kegan Paul plc
11 New Fetter Lane, London EC4P 4EE

Published in the USA by
Routledge & Kegan Paul Inc.
in association with Methuen Inc.
29 West 35th Street, New York, NY 10001

Set in 11/12pt Times
by Columns of Reading
and printed in Great Britain
by T.J. Press (Padstow) Ltd
Padstow, Cornwall

© *Institute for Policy Studies, World Hunger Year, and Joseph N. Belden 1986*

Library of Congress Cataloguing in Publication Data

Dirt rich, dirt poor.

(Alternate policies for America)
'The Institute for Policy Studies – world hunger year.'
Bibliography: p.
Includes index.
1. Agriculture and state – United States.   2. Nutrition
policy – United States.   3. Food relief – United States.
I. Belden, Joseph N.   II. Institute for Policy Studies.
III. Series.
HD1761.D55   1986   338.1'9'73   85-8274

British Library CIP Data available
ISBN 0-7102-0378-0 (c)
ISBN 0-7102-0666-6 (p)

Contents

Series editor's preface

The 'Alternative Policies for America' series offers a concrete set of programs for dealing with the country's most pressing domestic problems. It answers, in very specific terms, what radical analysts of the failure of the U.S. economic and social system can offer in the way of alternatives. We seek to make clear that there are ways of ensuring that all Americans can have a decent standard of material well-being and public services, a healthy and safe environment, and real participation in the political processes of governance and how goods and services are provided. The problem, this series attempts to show, is not the inability to create workable alternatives, but our system's unwillingness to effect the basic economic, social and political changes in the structure of American society that will permit such alternatives to take root. Books in the series will treat housing, food, technology, health, transportation, the environment, education, energy, bureaucracy, and democratic participation.

The Institute for Policy Studies sees this intellectual work as a first and necessary step in building a movement for political change. The analyses and ideas put forward in these books must take concrete form as demands for change at the federal, state and community levels. In many cases, model legislation embodying the proposals put forth here are being developed for introduction into the policy debate, and as a means of public education and constituency-building. The many individuals and groups who have been involved in the discussions and review which led to these books provide the nucleus for a continually expanding circle of activists who, we hope, some day will turn these ideas and proposals into a more just and humane America.

Chester Hartman
Institute for Policy Studies
Washington, D.C.

About the authors

Joe Belden is a specialist in rural issues who has worked for World Hunger Year; the Center for the Study of Social Policy; the Office of the Secretary, U.S. Department of Agriculture; the Committee on Agriculture, U.S. House of Representatives; and other public agencies and private groups.

Vincent Wilber is a former legislative assistant for foreign affairs, U.S. Senate, and Director of Public Affairs for the Agency for International Development. Earlier he covered the State Department for United Press International and was later assigned to Nicaragua, Brazil, Guyana and Denmark as a foreign service officer.

When the chapter on food assistance was written, its authors were all staff of the Food Research and Action Center, a nonprofit food-programs advocacy group. They include Enid Kassner, Elderly Nutrition Specialist; Rus Sykes, Director of Field Work; Ed Cooney, Child Nutrition Specialist; Lynn Parker, Nutritionist; Alan Sanders, Maternal and Child Health Specialist; Cynthia Schneider, Food Stamp Attorney; and Marsha Simon, Food Stamp Specialist.

Acknowledgments

This book has several authors. Vince Wilber wrote Chapter 5. A group of experts from the Food Research and Action Center – Enid Kassner, Rus Sykes, Ed Cooney, Lynn Parker, Alan Sanders, Cynthia Schneider and Marsha Simon – co-authored Chapter 4. And Joe Belden is responsible for Chapters 1, 2, 3 and 6.

Completion of the book would not have been possible without the assistance of a number of very able people. First among them are Catherine Lerza and Chester Hartman, who edited the entire manuscript for both style and content. Bill Ayres and Jack Clark of World Hunger Year and Chester Hartman of the Institute for Policy Studies provided the original impetus for the book through a joint effort of their respective organizations.

Mary Painter edited the first draft and helped with manuscript production. Carol Medlin provided research assistance on agricultural and environmental issues. Stratford Caldecott of Routledge & Kegan Paul offered encouragement and advice from the publisher's side.

Participants in two early meetings – of an advisory group in Washington and of a smaller subgroup assembled at Rodale Press – provided useful and constructive guidance on substance. Members of the advisory group included Nancy Amidei; Joe Brooks, Emergency Land Fund; Bill Burns, United Food and Commercial Workers; Fred Buttel, Cornell University; John Cavanagh, Institute for

Policy Studies; Jim Chapin, World Hunger Year; Kate Clancy, Syracuse University; Susan DeMarco, Texas Department of Agriculture; Arthur Domike, American University; Carol Tucker Foreman; Michael Goldhaber, Institute for Policy Studies; Kathy Goldman, Community Food Resource Center; Walt Grazer; Bob Gray, American Farmland Trust; Ellen Haas, Public Voice; Rebecca Harrington, Texas Farmworkers Union; Ferd Hoefner, Interfaith Action for Economic Justice; Frances Moore Lappé, Institute for Food and Development Policy; Cathy Lerza, Rural Coalition; Martin McLaughlin, Interfaith Action for Economic Justice; Jim Miller, National Grange; Agnes Molnar, Community Food Resource Center; Robert Rodale, Rodale Press; Susan Sechler; Larry Simon, Oxfam-America; Alan Stone, U.S. House Committee on Children, Youth and Families; and Marty Strange, Center for Rural Affairs. (Organizations are listed for purposes of identification only.)

The Rodale Press meeting benefited from the advice of several Rodale and Cornucopia Project staff members, including Richard Harwood, Medard Gabel and Helene Hollander.

Robert Rodale, Steve Haft and the Bydale Fund generously provided financial support without which the book could neither have been begun nor completed.

Finally, the life and the memory of Harry Chapin have inspired both the book and the ongoing work which must accompany it.

1 Introduction: The continuing crisis

The American food system is in crisis. That sentence or one very like it has introduced the hundreds of books, articles, reports, bills, laws and debates about food and agriculture of the last century. Such a sentence could have been written in the 1980s, the 1930s or the 1880s, and to an outsider it sounds like the little boy who cried wolf: the food system is always in deep trouble.

But what is the perennial problem? Why the crisis? On the face of it, the problem is a paradox. A growing number of Americans suffer hunger and malnutrition because of recent, severe federal budget cuts and an uncertain economy. On the production side, farm surpluses grow, and, consequently, depress farm income. At the same time, middle-income consumers confront a bewildering array of food products on their supermarket shelves. Many of these products have been so processed that they no longer resemble food. While paying a high price for these 'foods,' all consumers are affected by diet-related diseases.

This plenty in the midst of hunger, and disease in the midst of affluence, shows that policy has failed in all areas. During the 1970s, federal domestic feeding programs helped to reduce hunger, but since 1981 these programs have been cut back – with a resultant rise in hunger, malnutrition and infant mortality.

For fifty years, government policy has tried to protect the farm sector. Success has been incomplete at best, but in

1982 and 1983, support programs, especially the payment-in-kind (PIK) program, were disastrous. The farm program price tag reached $34 billion in 1983, but most of the benefits of PIK went to the very largest farm operators – those who needed it least. The program was a bail-out for the rich, financed by the taxpayer at enormous public cost. At the same time, mid-sized farmers were forced out of farming in record numbers.

Hunger and a depressed farm economy are only the most obvious examples of the problems of the food system, short- and long-term. Beneath these headline-grabbers are other continuing difficulties in the food system – increasing concentration of economic power at all levels, growing resource constraints and environmental degradation, declining food quality and nutritional standards, starvation and malnutrition abroad as well as at home, and inequity for workers in the system.

The present U.S. food system does not benefit producers, food industry workers or consumers. Policy-makers and activists concerned about these problems need to examine them in a new way. Many groups and individuals have formulated pieces of a solution in the past. Others have concentrated on rearguard actions to defend existing programs.

But what is needed is an overall reform of all parts of food policy. The intensifying problems of the 1980s – problems rooted both in decades of neglect and in recent failures – may soon become irreversible. In 1985, Congress took up its quadrennial rewriting of the major farm and food laws. Some progress was made in 1985, but not enough. The growing need for change in many areas continues to set the stage for a fundamental re-examination of policy.

Problems in the system

The American food system is, from a traditional perspecive, a wonder of productivity and efficiency. The history of twentieth-century agriculture seems to be a continuous march of progress – increasingly efficient farmers using new technologies to provide more than enough food for an expanding population, creating so much surplus that it cannot all be sold or even given away at home or abroad. Some statistics point to the astounding capacities of this food-producing machine. In 1900, about 38 percent of the labor force worked in agriculture, while today less than 3 percent of the work force labors on farms. This tiny group produces literal mountains of food and fiber. Government surplus warehouses bulge with dairy products; grain is left unsold in huge heaps; and many fruit and vegetable crops are left to rot in the fields because market prices are too low to make harvest and sale profitable. On top of this American farmers now export 30 percent of their total production – up from 10 percent in the 1950s.

This prodigious efficiency would seem to indicate that the eons-old battle with starvation is over, at least in rich countries, many of which produce enough to help feed hungry people in poorer nations. But this picture of abundance is not as rosy as it appears. Beneath the surface are a number of problems which are intimately linked with how and why the food system has changed in this century and with the role of government in those changes.

Some of the most important problems are related to the control of agricultural production:

- Farmers in the 1980s face hard times not seen since the 1930s. Income fell very sharply in 1980-82 after a record year in 1979, and has continued to drop.
- Bad times mean that farm debt has increased. Farm loan delinquencies and foreclosures are increasing. In mid-1984, more than 40 percent of the U.S. Department of Agriculture's Farmers Home Administration loans were delinquent. The $216 billion farm debt of 1983 – up from $29 billion in 1970 – could triple to $600 billion by 1990.

- Farmers are growing older and fewer in number. In the mid-1930s there were over six million farms; today there are about 2.4 million. Seven of every ten farmland owners in 1978 were over fifty years of age, an indication that younger people may not be available to step into the places of their elders in a few years, assuming that the young could afford to make the leap.
- Average farm size has been increasing rapidly. In 1940, the average farm was 175 acres. By 1974 farm size averaged 388 acres, and by 1981 the average was 429 acres.
- Related to farm debt is the now overwhelming cost of starting out in agriculture – an investment of at least $750,000 for a viable, mid-sized operation. Without riches in the bank or an inherited farm, it is almost impossible for young people to get into farming as farm owners, regardless of their skill or experience.
- Economic control of agriculture is becoming more and more concentrated. About 20 percent of all farms account for approximately 80 percent of total farm sales. Less than 3 percent of the nation's population owns all the agricultural land. Farmers also are increasingly controlled by a dwindling number of inputs suppliers and a dwindling number of buyers for their products.
- Absentee investors and large non-farm corporations own an increasing percentage of agricultural resources – land, equipment, livestock and other assets. Fed by incentives in the tax code, outside investment in agriculture puts real farmers who depend on agriculture for their livelihood at a growing disadvantage.
- Seasonal migrant agricultural laborers are among the nation's most underprivileged groups. Poorly protected by federal and state laws, these three million workers have made some advances in recent years but still face low wages, dangerous working conditions, employer hostility to labor organizing, and competition from undocumented workers. Even where protections exist,

employers frequently ignore them.
- Farm poverty remains a mostly invisible but persistent reality. The poverty rate for farm residents in 1982 was 22.1 percent, as compared to 14.8 percent for the non-farm population. Fifty-one percent of the black farm population and 60 percent of the Hispanic farm population were poor in 1982.

Another group of problems has to do with control of food marketing:

- Economic concentration in the food manufacturing and processing industries is increasing. The 50 biggest firms in food manufacturing increased their control of industry assets from 36 percent in 1950 to 64 percent in 1978. Farmers lose out when they must sell to market-dominating processors, and consumers lose too. Consumer overcharge due to economic concentration in food manufacturing amounts to $15 billion a year. Farmers make on average only about 40 cents of each dollar spent on food; the rest goes to the marketer.
- Food retailing is also moving toward greater economic concentration. In 1948, grocery chains of more than 100 stores controlled 27 percent of sales. By 1977 this control had increased to 41 percent. At the same time, technological changes in this industry threaten jobs.

A third set of food-system problems has to do with natural resources and the environment:

- Agriculture is dependent on energy inputs, particularly those that are fossil-fuel based. Modern production techniques require large doses of diesel fuel, oil and gasoline, electricity, natural gas and other sources of energy to power vehicles and machinery, produce fertilizer and pesticides, dry and store crops, and transport food. As the costs of the resources needed for production and marketing rise and their availability declines or becomes uncertain, farming creeps further out on the limb of energy dependence. In fact, if all the earth's food were raised using U.S.-style, energy-intensive methods, known world petroleum reserves would be exhausted in only thirteen years.

- Each year about three million acres of the country's 540-million-acre cropland base are lost to housing construction, commercial and industrial development, water projects, lakes and highways. The best agricultural land – flat, well-watered and drained – also happens to be ideal for suburban housing, industry and shopping centers. In areas of population growth, food production is moving farther and farther away from its ultimate users.

- Wind and water erosion destroy almost 6.5 billion tons of topsoil each year. About one-third of the topsoil base has been lost over the last 200 years.

- American agriculture in many parts of the nation, particularly in the West, is based on elaborate irrigation systems. Once surface water met most of the irrigation demand, but now ground water (i.e., underground) supplies are being tapped and, in some areas, depleted.

- Agriculture also places a great deal of stress on the environment and human health. Livestock feedlots and the heavy use of fertilizers cause water pollution. Pesticides are a health hazard to the farmer and are ultimately self-defeating, as their target species develop resistance to commonly used pesticides and as the poisons kill off natural pest predators. Continuous planting of the same crop year after year (monoculture) depletes soil nutrients and leads to escalating dependence on chemical fertilizers.

A fourth group of issues involves food consumption.

- Many Americans overeat or consume poor-quality diets. The now defunct Senate Select Committee on

Nutrition and Human Needs recommended in 1977 that people consume less fat, sugar and salt, and more grains, vegetables and fruits. The food industry vehemently opposed this common-sense approach to diet, and since 1981 the U.S. Department of Agriculture (USDA) and Congress have not publicized these recommendations.

- Food safety and quality are also problems for consumers. Since 1970, the number of additives in our food has risen 40 percent – 27,000 additives are now in use. Current federal labeling and testing regulations are inadequate to protect human health.

- Hunger in the United States is on the rise, as a result of the deep budget cuts made in food programs since 1981. Food stamp benefits amount to only about 43 cents per meal for each of the 22 million people now receiving them, while many of the 35 million people now living in poverty are not even on the program. More than $5 billion was cut from the food stamp program in 1981 and 1982.

A final area of concern is international trade and development assistance:

- During the 1970s, foreign demand for U.S. farm products grew about 8 percent per year. In 1960, about 10 percent of U.S. commodities was exported, but by 1980 this had grown to 28 percent. In today's plummeting farm economy, the constant cry is for more exports. Increased exports are seen as *the* solution. Yet it is foolish to rely on trade as a solution to domestic farm problems. Demand is uncertain, and the crops needed for an extensive export program will mean production on marginal land, leading to overuse of resources like soil and water. Exports also can compete with indigenous agricultural production in importing countries, and most international trade is controlled by giant multi-national corporations.

● Each year 40 million people, most of them children, die of starvation or diet-related diseases. Hundreds of millions more go hungry. Yet adequate resources exist in every country to produce food for all. The problem is that land and other resources are used in less-developed countries to produce cash crops for export, rather than to raise food for the local populace.

In brief overview, those are the problems. Public policies are, in theory, addressing them – leaving us with the central question: Have those policies succeeded?

Food production is the most heavily subsidized sector of our economy. Government at all levels has long tried to promote food production and protect consumers. It is ironic that – at the federal level particularly – government is also the cause of many of the problems described in the preceding section.

In many government agriculture policies, a sort of schizophrenia is at work that results in programs operating at cross-purposes – and that end up hurting the very people they are supposed to help. Contradictions in the food system cannot be removed without eliminating this schizophrenia. To do this we must first explore the overall goals of the food system and U.S. food policy.

Goals for an equitable, regenerative and healthful food system

A preliminary step toward preparing a national food policy is laying out a set of specific goals. A statement of goals cannot be immutable; it should instead be dynamic, subject to amendment as circumstances change. But it should be founded on certain basic principles: equity, security, conservation and human health.

Economist John Lee of the U.S. Department of Agriculture has offered a simple parable to illustrate the value of long-range goal setting:

The story is told of three stonemasons who were asked what they were doing. The first replied, 'I am laying stone.' The second replied, 'I am building a wall.' The third, being a person of vision and purpose, replied, 'I am building a cathedral.' Perhaps a clearly articulated and well-understood food policy could help program managers see how the stones they lay and the walls they build are contributing to the larger cathedral – to a sound and productive food system and to the nutritional well-being of people here and abroad, present and future.[1]

Lee, who directs USDA's Economic Research Service, has also outlined a long list of food-policy goals:

- Adequate income and returns for producers
- Reduction of risk and uncertainty in agricultural production
- Managerial freedom
- Access to market information for both producers and consumers
- Competitive markets for farm products and fair market practices
- Security of the food supply
- Reasonable food prices
- Safe, wholesome and nutritious food
- A wide variety and choice of food
- Efficient use and conservation of natural resources
- Environmental quality
- An efficient and competitive structure for the food distribution system
- Adequate economic returns to the people and groups necessary for an efficient system
- Equitable distribution of economic returns and power.
- Resilience in the face of stress
- Access to food for all the population
- Consistency with other national economic goals and policies[2]

This is a challenging set of goals. Building on this, we can put forth a call for an equitable, regenerative, and healthful food system. What do those three adjectives mean? What would such a food system look like? How would it affect the economy and public policy?

What would an equitable food system look like? Food production and consumption are a major portion of our market-oriented economy. Some participants in that system are winners, while others are losers. We believe that a fundamental goal of food policy should be balancing out inequities in the system so that the gap between 'winners' and 'losers' is not a huge one. That means food assistance for the poor, income fairness for producers, an end to the bias toward the largest farm operators, fair prices for all consumers, justice for farm laborers, and a concern for minority rights in the food system.

A regenerative food system is one which can be sustained over the long term, one rooted in the conservation of its productive capacities. Agriculture is, in itself, a *regenerating* process, but in recent decades the U.S. food system has been an *extractive* one – using resources faster than it replaces them. Modern agricultural practices have put enormous stress on soil, water and mineral resources. We have come to rely excessively on fossil-based energy supplies. We have seen a dangerous narrowing of the genetic resource base of major food crops. And we have lost a large amount of farmland to other uses. Urgently needed is a shift toward practices that are more conserving of natural resources and less harmful to the environment. That shift is the best hope for achieving real food security.

Based on these concerns, a set of goals for the U.S. food system includes:

- *An abundant supply of food for the consumer at reasonable prices*. Throughout most of history, people struggled to secure enough food for survival. Agricultural policies were therefore designed to increase, aid or stimulate production. Food shortages were a real fear. But even today an adequate supply of food must remain the first goal of a production system.

● *A food system that is directed toward producing healthy, nutritious foods.* Today, the American food system is aimed at producing the most profitable consumer products possible; health considerations are secondary to concern about profit, as the early 1984 scare about the preservative EDB in grains demonstrated. Concern about agricultural systems must be accompanied by concern about the processes by which agricultural products are turned into consumer goods.

● *Adequate food assistance for those persons who otherwise cannot afford a nutritious diet.* Many people cannot afford to feed themselves or their families. This condition, intolerable in a wealthy society, dictates that an important policy objective should be feeding or helping to feed the poor. For some years, but particularly in the 1970s, this objective was pursued successfully through a series of federal food assistance programs. Since 1981, however, there has been a reversal of this policy, leading to the conclusion that this goal must be near the top of our list.

● *Economic and social equity for those who produce our food, including a profitable return for the farmer and justice for food industry and agricultural workers.* The food producer, too, has a stake in this system. And producer here means not just the farm operator, but the hired agricultural laborer and the food-processing and marketing worker as well. These key workers in the system should receive a just return for their labor.

● *Income stability and economic profit for the farmer.* Chronic economic instability has long plagued agriculture. A solution to the problem of boom-and-bust overproduction, which leads to depressed farm income, must be found. But solutions such as curbs on production must not lead to shortages, must be well planned, and must work well with other aspects of the economy.

- *Agricultural production primarily by a large number of small and moderate-sized farms that are widely dispersed and owned, and occupied by their operators.* Agriculture structure should be based on a system in which most labor, capital and management on the farm are provided by the farm family. The moderate-sized family farm – one owned and managed by those who work it – is preferable to larger or absentee-owned units for almost every reason – economic, social and philosophical.

- *Food production and distribution in ways leading to maximum natural resource conservation and minimal environmental damage.* This goal relates to concerns as varied as soil and water conservation, loss of prime farmland, energy use, genetic conservation and diversity, and use of farm chemicals. The food system must be less wasteful of resources and less destructive to human health and the environment.

- *A responsible contribution toward elimination of hunger, malnutrition and agricultural underdevelopment in the Third World.* We cannot separate ourselves or agriculture from the world as a whole. Just as hunger is an American problem, starvation on a vast scale is an international problem. The long-term solution to hunger is the development of agricultural self-sufficiency in all countries.

Hard tomatoes, hard questions

The making of farm and food policies over the last

half-century has mostly consisted of tinkering with the same set of tools and ideas. But in the mid-1980s, the accumulating problems are gathering momentum. Applying the old solutions will no longer work, and certainly slipping back – for example, slashing the food stamp program – is no solution. Programs that work need to be retained or restored. But where policy has not worked, new ideas, models and experiments are needed.

The hard questions about food and fiber – ones that cause political discomfort – have not been faced squarely by established policy-makers or their allies in academia. But advocates for progressive change have been equally negligent; the public-interest community has dealt instead with the political status quo. There has been little time for reflection on either long-term trends or the reigning mythology of food policy. Yet those difficult questions must be faced. The current period of policy failure makes that task both timely and urgent.

Some of the hard questions in food policy have been avoided or ignored for years, but they are worth asking *and* worth answering.

An overview

- Should the government get out of agriculture and out of the food system generally? Should society, through public policy, intervene in the food economy at all? If there is intervention, what is the rationale for it?
- Does the food system need more public planning mechanisms? Or fewer such tools? Are there any real planning mechanisms in place now? The U.S. has engaged in public and private economic planning for years (especially in food), but the problem is that it has been poor planning. It has been piecemeal, uncoordinated, often undesirable or ineffective, and frequently carried out for the wrong purposes.
- Is an unregulated market economy the best way of

deciding who produces and who eats? Should we allow the market to determine each participant's share of finite resources, even when the result is both chronic oversupply and hunger?

Production

● Today there are no farm ownership or size policies. Do we need them? Can we continue to encourage unlimited growth of farm size and at the same time hope to retain a large number of small and moderate sized operations? Do we need outright limits on farm size – or enhancements and incentives? Should certain types of farm asset ownership, such as non-family corporations or foreign ownership, be limited?

● Should we continue to assume that general economic growth in agriculture will benefit all producers equally? If not, do we need to target growth or profit?

● How do we solve what seem to be chronic farm income problems? Do we need fewer farmers? Higher food prices? Is it inevitable that farm operators will need some public support, or can they find profit in the marketplace?

● Should the economic system, influenced as it is by policy, reward capital investment in agriculture more than it does labor? Since not all farmers are land-owners, should policy support those who do the actual work of agriculture, rather than those who own the land?

Resources

● Should soil and water conservation standards for agriculture and other users be mandatory, just as air and water quality standards are? Who should pay for conservation? Can farmers be expected to conserve resources when doing so amounts to an economic penalty?

● How can we solve the problem of loss of agricultural land to other competing uses? Should certain prime farmlands be zoned for exclusive agricultural use?

● Do we need a complete re-examination of our approach to the use of purchased chemical, mechanical and energy inputs in agriculture? Can agriculture become a net energy producer rather than a net energy user? How can a smooth transition be made to a sustainable and regenerative agriculture?

● Do we need to rethink the whole concept of private property rights in agriculture? What rights and what responsibilities does property ownership confer? Should such rights protect misuse of the resources needed for future generations?

Consumption

● What can be done to control inflation in consumer food prices? Should prices be controlled directly?

● What better food safety, food quality and nutritional policies are needed? Do our food and farm policies in some cases encourage consumption of poor-quality food? Do we need to establish better links between agricultural production, food processing, and nutrition and health policies? Should food advertising be more closely regulated?

● How can we better control or limit monopoly economic power in the food manufacturing and food retailing industries?

The world

● Can we solve domestic farm surplus and income problems with more exports of commodities? Do we

need more public regulation of food exports?
- Should commodity futures trading be more closely regulated? Should it be eliminated?
- How can we balance the need for international food aid with the need for increased agricultural self-reliance in less developed countries?

And finally, the bottom line

- How do we pay for food and farm policies and programs?

Some of these questions may generate more controversy than solutions. But we must start somewhere – these questions should add new life to the farm policy debate, and cut through conventional rhetoric and wisdom. This book cannot answer all of the questions definitively. It offers analysis and some policy prescriptions. But the authors hope that it will help trigger a serious consideration of the fundamental issues raised herein.

2 Land and food: Who controls production and marketing?

The structure of American agriculture is changing. Farms are becoming fewer in number, larger in size, highly specialized in production, and more dependent on the non-farm sector. Old patterns of resource ownership, financing, and decision-making are breaking down.[1]

For most human history, the vast majority of people in every society worked in agriculture. Only very recently, and only in industrial countries, has the number of farmers shrunk to a small proportion of the total population. This sharp and, in historical terms, sudden shift in the way food is produced has had several causes and numerous consequences – some good, some bad. The system of food marketing has also changed radically in recent decades. This chapter examines both production and marketing.

Economies expanding in the wake of the industrial revolution needed a larger urban work force and most of these workers came from the countryside. At the same time, technology changed farming itself. The adoption of mechanical and, later, chemical technologies meant that a single farmer could cultivate much larger areas of land. But it has brought with it a host of new issues in agriculture.

Starting up and getting out: entry and exit

For half a century the total number of farmers and the

number of new entrants into agriculture have been falling. This leads us to an important question: Who will be tomorrow's farmers? In 1983 the average age of farmers in the United States was fifty-two, and 70 percent of agricultural operators were over fifty years of age in 1978. The reason for this is money – the cost of starting out in farming today at a moderate size and with modern equipment can exceed $750,000. Without lots of money in the bank or a farm in the family to inherit, the new entrant faces almost insurmountable barriers. A young person trying to buy or rent land also faces very stiff competition from investors seeking a haven in land-price inflation or tax shelters for non-farm income.

There is something of a financial double whammy at work here. In good times for farmers, when prices are high, land prices will rise, often to levels out of reach of the beginning operator. Speculators and investors will bid for the land because of its rapidly inflating value. But when times are bad, when farm prices fall, the new entrant will be unable to earn enough to meet the mortgage payments on the land, *and* investors seeking tax (as opposed to inflation) shelters will bid for the acreage. These tax-loss 'farmers' can benefit most from a negative return, since they want to turn an agricultural loss into a shelter for high non-farm incomes.

The cumulative impact is that a potential entrant faces a series of very high hurdles. As one expert sees it:

> Today, there is concern that there will be a limited supply of new entrants, and even if additional farmers can be effectively employed, the capital and other barriers to entry may be too great. Thus, farming would continue to become more concentrated in the hands of fewer, older farmers.[2]

Complicating the entry problem are both barriers and incentives to exit, factors which affect retirement or other reasons for departures from the sector. The availability of heirs or buyers, the likelihood of securing and keeping a non-farm job, shifts in life style, the value of a particular farm and other factors influence exit. And there is, of course, a circular effect. Exit barriers translate into entry barriers. Less land is available for potential new farmers.

One incentive for exit – the high value of good farmland – is a barrier to entry for young persons without substantial assets. A retiring farmer wants to sell his land for the best possible price. But the only buyers able to afford that price may be an already well-established farmer, a non-farm investor or a real-estate developer planning some 'higher' use for the land. The beginning or expanding small farmer, who wants the acreage for its agricultural potential alone, cannot compete.

A 1983 USDA report sums up the basic entry dilemma:

> increased asset values, negative cash flows, and depressed commercial returns can lead to formidable barriers to entry for new owner-operator farmers, except through inheritance or high-income off-farm employment. The issue of whether the family farm system can survive, or whether the farms of the next generation will be very differently organized, owned, and operated remains unresolved.[3]

Present policy

The Farmers Home Administration (FmHA) of the U.S. Department of Agriculture is the federal agency which deals most directly with new farmer entry. But FmHA's current record of lending does not reveal a positive impact on new farmer entry or expansion for small-scale operators.

When the agency was established in 1946, its charge was to provide loans to farmers who could not get commercial credit. But over the years, FmHA took on additional responsibilities in housing and rural development and in other agricultural lending programs. In addition, its farm lending activities became directed at larger operations. In 1978 Congress attempted to put at least some FmHA activities back on track. The Agricultural Credit Act of that year called for more agency support of low-equity and beginning farmers. The result was the 'limited resources' loan program, a requirement that some portion of FmHA farm ownership and operating loans be distributed at lower-than-market interest rates. This program could help new entrants and expanding small farmers. But it has never been fully implemented and has often been threatened by the budget cutters' knives.

Even fewer policies are designed to help exiting farmers. Only in inheritance taxation is there some connection, but it consists of an unfortunate conflict between entry and exit needs. Thanks to the Reagan/Congressional tax revolution of 1981, there soon will be no effective inheritance taxes on estates of less than $600,000. Even farm estates of a greater value will suffer little tax penalty. This situation is helpful to heirs, but it further stifles the ambitions of potential entrants. A stiffer inheritance tax might mean that some land would have to be sold to pay the Internal Revenue Service's bill – and that land might go to entering farmers.

New directions

A number of common-sense steps could help solve both the entry and the exit dilemmas.

First and foremost, the limited resource loan program of FmHA should be strengthened and expanded. The current limited resource allocation of 20 percent of ownership and operating loans should be extended to at least 40 percent. And the agency's overall mission should be reoriented to its historic purposes – help for the low-equity farmer who cannot obtain credit elsewhere.

Another idea is state or federal Beginning Farmer Assistance programs, which could complement the FmHA limited resource loan allocation. Beginning farmer programs create, through state-financed bonds or an allocation of funds from the state legislature, a loan fund which can be made available to new farmers. The money helps farmers purchase and equip a farm, and is often made available at preferential interest rates. Today, more than a dozen states have a Beginning Farmers Assistance Program, and the best of these – for example, in Iowa and Minnesota – are targeted to new farmers who could not otherwise get into agriculture. Several members of Congress have proposed a federal version of this program which would make available guaranteed loan funds to state government programs which meet specific criteria – most important, that the program serve those farmers who could not otherwise get started.

The current tax treatment of estates also should be reformed. Farms of a size large enough to capture maximum economies of scale, and farms smaller than that size, should pass to succeeding generations free of any inheritance taxation. But if larger than the level of maximum efficiency, farm estates should be taxed very steeply. This can help put land back on the market. But such a step must be taken in concert with other tax measures and controls on land ownership.

One practical approach to solving both entry and exit problems is found in two programs – one French, one Canadian – almost unknown in the United States. Both, in essence, acquire land from departing producers and lease or sell it to new entrants or expanding small-scale operators. The Canadian example is found in Saskatchewan, where a 1972 statute established a provincial land bank that buys available farm land on the open market and then leases it, with a future option to buy, to entering or expanding farmers. To be eligible for the program, a potential lessee must have a net worth of $60,000 or less and a net annual income of $10,000 or less.

In France, a similar program is run by the quasi-public Sociétés d'Aménagement Foncier et d'Establissement Rural (SAFER), local institutions which serve a 'land banking' function. The SAFERs buy farmland, improve it, and resell to small farmers desiring enlargement or consolidation or to young persons trying to enter. Between 1964 and 1975, the SAFERs bought 2.1 million acres and resold 1.8 million. Land is bought in open competition or it may be acquired by right of pre-emption. This process is specifically intended to keep good land in agriculture.

Big farm, little farm: land ownership and farm size

Entry is only the tip of the iceberg of production problems – perhaps the most fundamental of these problems are land ownership and farm size. Consider a few facts:

- In 1981, the top 5 percent of the country's farms – those with annual sales of $200,000 or more – accounted for 49 percent of total farm sales. Thirteen percent of the farms – those with grosses of $100,000 per year and up – had 68 percent of the sales. At the other end of the scale, farms with less than $20,000 in sales in 1981 accounted for 60 percent of the total number of operations, but only 7 percent of sales.
- Farm size has been increasing steadily for decades, although it appears to have stabilized recently. In 1950 the average farm was 213 acres. By 1970 this figure was up to 374 acres, and in both 1980 and 1981 it was 429 acres.
- Farm numbers have declined steadily since the mid-1930s, although they have stabilized recently:

	Numbers of farms
1950	5,648,000
1960	3,963,000
1970	2,949,000
1980	2,428,000
1981	2,436,000

- In 1920, the 32 million people living on farms made up 30 percent of the nation's population. But by 1979 only

3 percent of the population (6.2 million persons) were farm residents.

● Less than 3 percent of the nation's population owned all farmland in 1978. Five percent of the farmland owners – about 0.14 percent of the total population – owned 48 percent of the agricultural acreage. One percent of the farmland owners own 30 percent of the total acreage. One percent – 337,000 persons – of the owners of all the private land, including farm acreage, own almost 50 percent of that land (648 million acres), an average of 1,923 acres each.

● Less than 7 percent of the farms account for more than 54 percent of all the land in farms.

TABLE 1 *U.S. farms by total numbers and sales class, 1981*

Sales class					
	Under $10,000	*$10,000 $39,999*	*$40,000 $99,999*	*$100,000 $199,999*	*$200,000 and over*	*Total*
No. of farms	1,178,000	564,000	396,000	186,000	112,000	2,436,000
Percent of total farms	48	23	16	8	5	100
Percent of total farm sales	4	9	19	19	49	100

Source: David Harrington *et al.*, *U.S. Farming in the Early 1980s: Production and Financial Structure*, USDA, ERS, Ag. Econ. Rept. 504, September 1983, p. 3.

What these and other statistics show is that farms are becoming fewer in number and larger in size. Ownership and market domination are becoming increasingly concentrated among a relatively small number of farms. At the bottom are a very large number of small farms and rural residences with low sales levels. But most of the operators of the rural residences and some on the small farms do not rely solely on agriculture for income. They have off-farm jobs and may be less susceptible to farm price fluctuations than the full-time operators. Caught in the middle are many of the small and medium-size operators. Most of these farms have difficulty competing with the large farms, but they are not small enough to function as only part-time operations.

In some commodities – cattle feeding, for example – concentration has become particularly acute. Farmer feedlots, as defined in a 1983 USDA study, are those with a capacity of 1,000 head of cattle or less. Larger-capacity operations are called commercial feedlots. The study indicates that in 1964, 61.3 percent of fed cattle sales were from farmer feedlots, with an average of 49 head sold per feedlot. Commercial feedlots, averaging 4,297 head sold, accounted for 38.7 percent of sales. By 1981, these shares had more than reversed themselves. Farmer feedlots accounted for 26.7 percent of cattle sold, while commercial lots had 73.3 percent. The average number of head sold per lot in 1981 was 60 for the farmer operations (an 18 percent increase from 1964) and 7,524 for the commercial lots (a 75 percent increase). The total number of farmer feedlots also declined sharply – from 217,680 in 1964 to 102,168 in 1981. Just since 1978, the number of farmer feedlots fell by 23,000 – from 125,523 to 102,168. Commercial feedlots grew in number from 1,564 in 1964 to 2,241 in 1981.[4]

This very sharp trend is not reflected in every other type of farm, but the general message is still the same – the way our food is produced has changed drastically in just a few years. This picture also differs from the popular image of the yeoman farmer, the small operator. There are still many such units, but they produce very little.

The biggest farms have grown very rapidly, while the smallest have been declining in number. Between 1970 and 1980, the number of farms by sales class increased or declined in the following manner:

Sales:	*Percent change in number of farms*[5]
$200,000 and over	+535%
$100,000-$199,999	+400%

$40,000-$99,999	+136%
$20,000-$39,999	−8%
$10,000-$19,999	−21%
Under $10,000	−43%

Data on ownership are less complete. In fact, a real problem for policy-makers is that very little is known about who owns the nation's farmland. But the little that is known is disturbing. For example, in 1978 there were some six million owners of farmland. This is only a slight drop from the number of farmland owners in 1946, the last year in which ownership was surveyed. But there has been a very large decline in the proportion of owner-operators (those who both own and manage their own land). In 1946, 70 percent of the owners of farmland were farm operators. But by 1978 only one-third of the owners operated their farms.[6] This is evidence of a pronounced shift toward absentee ownership and hired management. Is this important? It may be, because as a nation we have usually desired widespread ownership of land among the largest possible number of holders.

It also may be surprising to learn that maximum economies of size are achieved by relatively small farms. A 1981 study by economists at the U.S. Department of Agriculture examined wheat, feed grains and cotton farms in seven regions of the country. Two major findings stand out:

- On average the most efficient farm had not millions in gross income but a sales level of $133,000 and an acreage of 1,157.
- A farm with $46,000 in sales and 322 acres was large enough to provide 90 percent of the maximum economies of size.

The study further concluded that

Since medium size commercial farms achieve most technical

cost efficiencies, society benefits little in terms of lower real food costs from further increases in farm size. Actually, many commercial farms now exceed the size necessary to achieve all available cost efficiencies.[7]

What this means is that a larger farm is not necessarily the most efficient producer of food. Despite this fact, the 13 percent of all farms with 1981 sales of $100,000 or more totalled 68 percent of farm sales.

Continuing along the present path will result in greatly increased concentration. In fact, a 1980 USDA study predicts that by the year 2000:

- The total number of farms will have fallen to 1,750,000 – down from 2,375,000 in 1982.
- The largest one percent of all farms will sell almost half of all farm products.
- The largest 50,000 operations will account for 63 percent of total cash receipts, as compared to 30 percent in 1969.
- The 50,000 largest farms will operate 50 percent of the farmland, as contrasted with 30 percent in 1969.
- Farms with sales of $100,000 or more will account for 96 percent of total production, compared to 35 percent in 1969.
- Farms with sales of $500,000 and up will market an astounding 77 percent of total production, as compared to 20 percent in 1969.[8]

What does this mean to those of us who aren't farmers? Isn't this just the way the economic pie gets sliced? It's not that simple – and that's where public policies come in.

Present policy

Few, if any, policies limit farm size and ownership. But many public policies have done the opposite. Over many years some programs have indirectly caused concentration in ownership and growth in farm size. Later sections of this chapter will address credit, tax and commodity price-support programs – all of which have promoted concentration because they remove a considerable amount of risk from farming. They encourage existing farmers to expand and entice non-farm investors into agriculture. While government programs are not the sole cause of concentration, they at least can be changed by a concerned public.

Historically, there have been specific public policies which dealt with farm size. But they were for the most part ignored or repealed. The Homestead Act of 1862 was created to allow for agricultural settlement of the American Midwest and West. Applicants were allowed a maximum of 160 acres at a cost of $1.25 an acre. The Reclamation Act of 1902 offers federal support for irrigation projects in 17 Western states. The availability of water has turned deserts into lush fruit and vegetable farms. In the original act no irrigation aid was to go to farms of more than 160 acres in size. But this provision was circumvented for decades and finally rewritten in 1982. The new provision increases the limit to 960 acres but raises the charges for irrigation water.

One still operative law addressing farm size is in the farm price support programs. There is a $50,000 limit on direct support payments to any single individual. But some participants in the programs have been able to circumvent this restriction by having each of several individuals be responsible for raising different crops on the same farm. Thus one farm ends up over the payment limit. Most operations do not reach the ceiling anyway, however. For example, participating farmers with more than 2,500 acres in 1978 averaged $36,005 in payments.[9]

New directions

A new policy on farm size and farmland ownership could regain some of the ground lost in recent years and lead to more dispersed land ownership patterns and a larger number of moderate-size farms. Several recommendations follow:

- Target agricultural price-support benefits to family farms large enough to achieve most significant economies of size and earn an adequate family income. Beyond the level needed to achieve efficiency, supports should be phased down or eliminated.
- Restrict price-support program benefits to farms that are actively managed and operated by their owners.
- Limit farm ownership by non-family farm corporations and foreign purchasers. Today, ten states have laws which limit corporate ownership, and North Dakota and Nebraska ban corporate ownership outright.
- Amend the recently weakened 1902 Reclamation Act to strike some compromise between the old 160-acre limit and the present standard.
- Establish a land bank for purchase of available farm-land, with resale or lease in moderate-size parcels. (See the preceding section on entry for details.)

Outright limits on farm size may be too controversial for consideration in the U.S., but some other countries have already imposed such restrictions. For example, in Denmark a farm can be no larger than 75 hectares (185 acres). Regulation of ownership by outside investors and large non-agricultural firms will probably be easier for Americans to swallow. At the least, we should not provide public support in the form of price programs, cheap credit or tax relief to farms that are considerably larger than the size needed for maximum efficiency.

Minority ownership: the disappearing black farmer

Black-operated farms are rapidly disappearing. Between 1900 and 1978, the number of black farms declined by 94 percent, while the number of white-operated farms fell by 56 percent. The most recent numbers show that between 1969 and 1978 the number of black-operated farms fell from 134,000 to 57,000. And in the same period the land in black farms fell from 6.2 million to 4.2 million acres. In the peak year of 1920, there were 926,000 farms owned or run by blacks – one in seven U.S. farms. But by 1978, only 57,000 farms – 6.2 percent of that 1920 total – remained, and black operations as a proportion of all farms had fallen to one in forty-five. Between 1970 and 1980, the black farm population declined by 65 percent, while the white farm population declined by 22 percent. Blacks now comprise only 4 percent of the nation's farm population.

At the current rate of loss, virtually no blacks will own farms in this country by the end of the next decade. It may be tempting to suggest that, since many black farm families are low income and most are in the South, movement out of agriculture and into urban areas is a positive step. Such a movement from Southern rural areas to Northern cities did indeed occur and is still occurring; it is in fact the major demographic shift for black Americans in the twentieth century. For some the experience may have been beneficial. But for others, it meant the transformation of rural poverty into urban poverty. Many blacks who migrated to the inner cities found overcrowded and substandard housing, welfare dependence, crime, drug abuse and other problems. Black farmers and their families met discrimination and found little demand for their labor in Northern cities.

A U.S. Civil Rights Commission study of black land loss found that

> as a result of the opportunity for self-employment, managerial experience, and considerably enlarged discretion over their lives, black landowners are more self-reliant, better off nutritionally, more secure psychologically, and more confident of the future than black non-owners.[10]

Over the last century no other population group has suffered a similar loss of farmland. America is moving very quickly toward a situation in which whites will own almost all of the agricultural assets of the country, a situation that could have serious consequences for race relations.

Present policy

The rapid loss of black-operated farms would be bad enough had it been caused solely by market forces and personal choice. But the truth is that the federal government has mostly ignored and sometimes acted against the interests of small-scale black farmers. The principal culprit has been the Farmers Home Administration. The Civil Rights Commission study pointed out

> [that USDA has been] . . . instrumental in raising the economic, educational and social levels of thousands of farm and rural families. . . .
>   [But a] quarter of a million Negro families stand as a glaring exception to this picture of progress.[11]

The Commission found that FmHA did not provide services to black farmers comparable to those provided to whites. Discrepancies occurred in sizes of loans, the purposes for which the loans were made, and provision of technical assistance. Recently FmHA assistance to blacks has declined. For example, FmHA loans to blacks fell from 19.6 percent of all agency loans in 1972 to 8 percent in 1983. With regard to the needs of black farmers, the Commission also found FmHA staff training and outreach limited, compliance reviews cursory, and data collection inadequate.

New directions

A number of steps could help curb the loss of black farmers and perhaps even draw some back to the land. Some suggestions:

● Reform FmHA practices and target funding. Provide more training to FmHA personnel in the needs of black farmers, more outreach to black farmers, and increased funding for the limited resource loan program (See the credit section below for more on this last point). Specific percentages of FmHA farm loan funds should be earmarked for black operators in states where black population is concentrated.
● Strengthen extension and training programs for black farmers, and devote more agricultural research to the needs of such farmers. Increased support for the predominantly black land grant colleges would be a useful way to achieve this end.
● Provide more marketing advice to black farmers.
● Ensure that low-income rural black families have adequate assistance in preparing wills and dealing with other legal matters in order to prevent the loss of farmland. This advice can come from a strengthened program of legal services for the poor and from properly trained extension and FmHA personnel.

Mortgage on the future: money and credit

A key to land ownership and to continuing farm operation is access to credit. Like other businesses in the American economy, agriculture needs financing. In fact, agriculture has become capital-intensive and is becoming more so each year. But most farmers are overcapitalized, deeply in debt and out on a financial limb.

Once farmers used relatively little borrowed capital. In 1940, as Table 2 shows, total farm debt, including government price-support loans, was only $10 billion. But by 1983, debt hit $216.3 billion, an amount larger than recent federal budget deficits.

TABLE 2 *Total farm debt, selected years, 1940-83*

	Farm debt		
Year	Real-estate	Non-real-estate	Total
	(in millions of dollars)		
1940	$ 6,586	$ 3,449	$ 10,034
1950	5,579	6,875	12,454
1960	12,082	12,693	24,775
1970	29,183	23,844	53,027
1975	44,637	37,006	81,643
1980	85,421	80,382	165,803
1983*	109,507	106,812	216,319

*Preliminary.
Source: USDA, ERS, *Economic Indicators of the Farm Sector*: *Income and Balance Sheet Statistics 1982*, ECIFS 2-2, October 1983, p. 118.

An explanation for this sharp increase in debt load lies in the changes that have taken place in agriculture. Farmers used to produce many of their own inputs. Feed raised on the farm nourished draft animals, and the animals in turn provided the power to till the fields. But today, farmers purchase most or all of their inputs. They must pay for machinery, fuel, seed, fertilizers, pesticides and household necessities. Today the rural family buys groceries at the supermarket and other necessities at a nearby shopping mall. In fact, as consumers farm families are now very much like urban and suburban families.

Table 2 shows that the increase in agricultural debt has accelerated in recent years. Between 1940 and 1970, the figure increased five-fold. But, in the thirteen years between 1970 and 1983, the total more than quadrupled. Since 1975, total debt has almost tripled. Non-real-estate borrowing for operating expenses has been increasing more rapidly than has real-estate borrowing.

More disturbing is that the liquidity of agriculture is declining. Faced with increases in both land prices and operating costs, and driven on by the incentive of borrowing against inflated land values, farmers have overextended their use of credit. The debt-to-asset ratio – an index which compares agriculture's borrowing with its total worth – has been increasing sharply. In 1950, this ratio was 9.3 percent (on a per-farm average basis), but by 1983 it was up to 20.6 percent. (See Table 3).

TABLE 3 *Farm assets, liabilities and debt-to-asset ratio, average per farm, January 1, selected years, 1950-83*

Year	Total assets	Total liabilities	Debt-to-asset
	(in dollars)		*ratio*
1950	$ 23,823	$ 2,205	9.3
1960	53,036	6,252	11.8
1970	106,780	17,981	16.8
1980	414,117	68,288	16.5
1983*	437,016	90,133	20.6

*Preliminary.
Source: USDA, ERS, *Economic Indicators of the Farm Sector: Income and Balance Sheet Statistics 1982*, ECIFS 2-2, October 1983, p. 104.

Agriculture has greatly increased its degree of financial leverage and has thus become highly vulnerable to variations in income. Fixed costs combined with fluctuations in weather and international trade mean farmers face a stable or rising schedule of expenses (including interest payments) and an unstable, boom-bust income situation. This financial overextension has become so extreme that, in 1982, net farm income barely covered interest payments on agricultural debt. This dangerous situation has been building for several years as the gap between income and interest payments closes. In good years, such as 1979 and 1981, income may be considerably higher than debt payments, but not every year is a good one, as Table 4 shows.

TABLE 4 *Interest payments as a percentage of net farm income*

Year	Net farm income	Interest payments on farm debt	Interest as a percentage of income
	(in millions of dollars)		
1940	$ 4,482	$ 479	10.7
1950	13,648	598	4.4
1960	11,518	1,374	11.9
1970	14,381	3,381	23.5
1979	32,251	13,078	40.5
1980	21,505	16,261	75.6
1981	30,058	19,864	66.0
1982	22,051	21,829	98.9

Source: USDA, ERS, *Economic Indicators of the Farm Sector: Income and Balance Sheet Statistics 1982*, ECIFS 2-2, October 1983, p. 104.

The result is bankruptcy and foreclosure for an increasing number of farm operators. Larger farms are much more likely to carry a sizeable debt load. Table 5 shows total and average debt per farm by sales class as of the beginning of 1983.

The farm debt is owed to a variety of lenders – the quasi-public Farm Credit System, the Farmers Home Administration, the Commodity Credit Corporation (CCC), private banks, life insurance companies, other private firms and individuals. Most lending does not come from government sources. In 1982, FmHA held 8.6 percent of real-estate and 15.6 percent of non-real-estate debt. The CCC lends only for non-real-estate expenses and held 8.6 percent of that total in 1982. Commercial banks, insurance firms, and 'individuals and others' accounted for 48.7 percent of real-estate debt. Banks and individuals and others (insurance

TABLE 5 *Total debt and average debt per farm, by sales class, January 1, 1983*

Sales class	Total farm debt (in millions)	Percent share	Average debt per farm (in dollars)
Less than $10,000	$17,758	8.2	$ 15,370
$10,000-$39,999	25,810	11.9	46,547
$40,000-$99,999	48,619	22.5	123,878
$100,000-$199,999	44,179	20.4	237,952
$200,000 and over	79,954	37.0	711,676

Source: USDA, ERS, *Economic Indicators of the Farm Sector: Income and Balance Sheet Statistics 1982*, ECIFS 2-2, October 1983, p. 136.

companies do not make non-real-estate loans) held 51.7 percent of non-real-estate debt. The Federal Land Banks of the Farm Credit system held 42.7 percent of real-estate debt in 1983, and the system's Production Credit Associations accounted for 23.1 percent of non-real-estate debt.

Present policy

Federal programs to support agriculture, most of which date from the 1930s and 1940s, were designed initially to serve small and moderate-size farms, the size that predominated at the time the programs began. But as agriculture has changed, and as farms have become larger, the programs also have changed. This is especially true for credit policy. Bigger farms now reap a large part – sometimes most – of the benefits of credit (and commodity) programs.

The 1981 USDA study of the structure of agriculture contends that credit policies have had both good and bad results. They have –

● Achieved the apparent objective of plentiful supplies of capital for farmers, at favorable rates and terms.
● But also contributed to an inefficient use of resources, an increased dependence on capital- and energy-intensive technology, inflation in land prices, and the concentration of production in the hands of fewer, larger farmers.[12]

Evidence also indicates that credit policy has benefited large farms at the expense of smaller ones.

The Farmers Home Administration is the most important public source of farm credit. FmHA has four principal programs for agriculture. They include farm ownership (FO), farm operation (OL), disaster emergency relief (EM), and economic emergency relief (EE). In fiscal year 1983, the total amount of loans and grants for all agency programs was $116 billion. Of this amount, $52 billion went to the four farm programs. Table 6 shows how that $52 billion breaks down.

Since 1978, a portion of FO and OL lending has been set aside for 'limited-resource' borrowers, those low-equity and beginning farmers who represent FmHA's original clients. The Reagan Administration has tried to eliminate the limited resource program, but Congress has persistently refused to do so. In fact, Congress has directed that at least 20 percent of both ownership and operating funds go to limited resource clients. These loans are available at a subsidized interest rate as a further aid to the low-equity farmer.

But the program has not been fully utilized. For

TABLE 6   *Farm program lending of the Farmers Home Administration, 1983*

Program	Number of loans	Dollar amount (in billions of dollars)
Farm operating loans	2,380,970	$14.2
Farm ownership loans	387,506	$10.1
Disaster emergency loans	1,184,457	$21.1
Economic emergency loans	121,000	$6.6

Source: USDA, Farmers Home Administration, *A Brief History of Farmers Home Administration,* March 1984, p. 19.

example, in fiscal year 1983, only 23.1 percent of FO dollars, and only 11.5 percent of OL funds, went to limited-resource borrowers. On a state by state basis, the level of compliance with the 20 percent requirement varied dramatically. For example, in FY 1983, Virginia directed only 2.5 percent of ownership loans to limited resource borrowers. In neighboring North Carolina, 25.1 percent of FO funds went to limited-resource farmers.[13]

Another change came to FmHA farm lending programs in the Agricultural Credit Act of 1978 – the same law that gave birth to the limited resource program – with creation of the economic emergency loan program growing out of the severe financial crisis affecting agriculture in the late 1970s. During that period, many farmers found themselves in economic trouble. The emergency program was designed to help all farmers, but it has mainly served larger farms. In 1979, 5.2 percent of OL loans, 5.4 percent of FO loans, but 34.7 percent of EE loans went to borrowers with gross farm sales of $100,000 and over. Almost 70 percent of the EE funds went to operations with $40,000 or more in sales.[14]

The Farm Credit System is not a public agency, but its cooperative member banks started out with federal funding and are regulated by a quasi-federal body, the Farm Credit Administration. Some observers feel that the FCS Federal Land Banks and Production Credit Associations serve large-scale farm operators. USDA's study on the structure of agriculture questioned whether the banks of the system have 'been too liberal in extending credit, thereby contributing to land-price inflation and further concentration in farming.'[15]

The USDA concluded that FCS may well have done just that. FCS has increasingly lent to absentee-owned, investor-rented farm operations, as well as to hobby farms where owners are employed full-time in lucrative non-agricultural jobs. The system's administrators point out that more than 20 percent of Land Bank loans go to producers under age 35. But most of these younger borrowers are relatively well-off. In 1970, for example, among borrowers who were under age 35, 24.5 percent of Land Bank debt, but only 5.2 percent of FmHA real-estate debt, was held by those who had farm sales of $40,000 or more.

New directions

Credit policy has made a significant contribution to increasing economic concentration in agriculture. This trend needs to be checked and reversed. To do this, federal credit programs must be returned to their original purposes.

Specific recommendations include:

● FmHA's limited-resource loan program should be retained and strengthened and funding increased. Measures are also needed to ensure that each state meets the mandated quota, and that all potential

FmHA borrowers are informed about the limited-resource program.

- The economic emergency loan programs, which primarily help larger farms, should be replaced with crop insurance or non-subsidized loans. Ending or reducing this program could reduce public spending for agriculture and contribute to reductions in the federal deficit. Some emergency funds could be shifted to the ownership and operating programs, however.
- No loans should go to farms larger than the size needed to achieve reasonable efficiency.
- Foreclosure proceedings on FmHA loans should protect all due process rights of borrowers. Deferral of delinquent payments should be granted when the borrowers have no control over their inability to repay.
- Loans with variable repayment schedules should be adopted as a method of helping small farm operators meet year-to-year interest payments. Such schedules could be linked to net farm income, allowing for high payments in good years and easier terms in bad years.
- The Farm Credit Act of 1980 requires that the Farm Credit System set up preferential programs for young, beginning and small-scale farmers. This requirement should be enforced. And at least 10 percent of FCS lending should go to young, beginning and small-scale applicants.
- FCS lending should be carefully targeted toward operators who reside on their farms, provide management and labor to the farm business, and earn most of their income from agriculture.

Commodities and farm income: a policy for boom-and-bust

Farmers earn their living by raising and selling crops. It sounds simple, but the very nature of agriculture adds a warehouse of monkey-wrenches to the situation. Farmers as a group are a very large number of producers selling to very few buyers. Farmers tend to overproduce, and volume of production is often dictated more by weather than by planting decisions. A bumper crop can often mean financial disaster for the farmer, since too much production means falling prices. Chronic farm surplus is in large part the result of advances in technology. Agricultural researchers and engineers, most of them publicly financed, are continually developing new and better technologies. Production on farms rises as the new methods are adopted, but there often is no market for the excess.

What gets produced? In 1982, total cash receipts for all farm marketing (including the net value of price-support loans) amounted to $144.6 billion. Table 7 indicates the dollar value of farm sales of major commodities.

Gross returns look large, but net returns to farmers are unstable and often low, making for a recurring saga of boom-and-bust. One bad year can mean the end for a farmer with years of experience.

Over the last ten years, agricultural income has continued on its roller coaster ride. Table 8 shows that when inflation is accounted for (i.e., using constant 1967 dollars), farm income has been dropping since 1973.

A net of $22.1 billion in 1981 current dollars was really only $7.6 billion in 1967 deflated dollars. That $7.6 billion was down from a peak (again in 1967 dollars) of $25.9 billion in 1973.

In real terms, net farm income in 1980 and 1982 hit its lowest levels since the early 1930s. Thus farming as a business venture seems to have made no progress in half a century – despite the presence of a set of federal programs aimed at solving the chronic problem of boom-and-bust.

Present policy

Since 1933, the centerpiece of agricultural policy has been the group of laws that make up the price-support programs. These farm programs, as they are commonly called, deal

TABLE 7 *Cash receipts from farm marketings (including net Commodity Credit Corporations loans) by major commodity, 1982*

Commodity	Cash receipts (in millions)
Livestock and products	$ 70,199
Cattle and calves	29,893
Dairy products	18,354
Hogs	10,623
Broilers	4,481
Eggs	3,436
Other	3,412
Crops	74,353
Corn	13,428
Soybeans	12,434
Wheat	9,777
Vegetables and melons	8,089
Fruits and nuts	6,669
Cotton	4,573
Tobacco	3,342
Other	16,041
Total	$144,551

Source: USDA, ERS, *Economic Indicators of the Farm Sector: Income and Balance Sheet Statistics, 1982*, ECIFS 2-2, October 1983, p. 21.

with individual commodities but do not cover all crops and livestock products. The most important commodities covered include wheat, feed grains (mostly corn), cotton, tobacco and rice. Dairy products and some fruits and vegetables are covered in separate marketing order programs.

Most of this policy structure was erected during the 1930s, although it has been modified, refined and amended constantly in the intervening years. The impetus for the programs came from a severe agricultural depression which began in the early 1920s and helped cause the Great Depression. Agriculture was devastated during these years.

TABLE 8 *Gross and net farm income and production expenses, 1940-81*

Year	Gross income from farming	Production expenses	Net farm income, current dollars*	Net farm income, 1967 dollars**
		(in millions of dollars)		
1940	11.3	6.8	4.5	10.7
1945	25.4	13.1	12.3	22.8
1950	33.1	19.5	13.6	18.9
1955	33.5	22.2	11.3	14.1
1960	38.9	27.4	11.5	13.0
1965	46.5	33.6	12.9	13.7
1970	58.8	44.5	14.4	12.4
1971	62.1	47.1	15.0	12.4
1972	71.2	51.7	19.5	15.6
1973	99.0	64.6	34.4	25.9
1974	98.3	71.0	27.3	18.5
1975	100.6	75.0	25.6	15.9
1976	102.9	82.7	20.1	11.8
1977	108.7	88.9	19.8	10.9
1978	127.2	99.5	27.7	14.2
1979	150.4	118.1	32.3	14.8
1980	150.1	128.6	21.5	8.7
1981	162.2	140.1	22.1	7.6

* Not adjusted for inflation
** Adjusted for inflation
Source: USDA, ERS, *Economic Indicators of the Farm Sector: Income and Balance Sheet Statistics, 1982*, ECIFS 2-2, October 1983, pp. 77, 79.

For example between 1925 and 1929, net farm income averaged $6.1 billion a year; but between 1930 and 1934, the average was only $3 billion a year.

Faced with this crisis, the new Roosevelt Administration moved quickly in the spring of 1933 to establish a new farm relief program. The Agricultural Adjustment Act, passed in 1933 only days after Franklin Roosevelt took office, was the first piece of New Deal legislation. This law and other legislative products of the 1930s have been changed and redirected over the years, but they remain today the major programs for farm income support.

There are three basic forms of support:

- *Loans* made to the farmer in advance of production and harvest. The farmer's future crop serves as collateral for the loan, the amount of which is determined according to a dollar value per unit of production. If the market price falls below the loan level, the producer can turn over the crop to the government and keep the loan. But if the market prices are higher than the loan rate, the farmer can sell, pay off the loan (with interest) and retain a profit.
- *Deficiency payments* made directly to the participating farmer as an income bridge between low market prices and established government 'target prices.' If the market price falls below the target price, the farmer receives the difference between the target and the loan rate or market price, whichever is lower. Loans and deficiency payments work in tandem and are available for wheat, feed grains and cotton. This program is usually activated in years of potential surplus and often in conjunction with acreage reduction programs aimed at cutting farm production in order to keep prices higher.
- *Marketing orders* through which producers and the government agree to restrict supplies of a particular commodity, improving prices by keeping surplus off the market. Others cover certain regions in which a crop is produced, and supply restriction is achieved through standards for size and quality. Producers vote on whether to approve the establishment of a marketing order. Once approved, all producers of the commodity are bound by the order's restrictions. Milk and a number of fruits and vegetables are covered by marketing orders.

These three programs are among the oldest and most permanent federal policy tools. But there are also other programs. Two are important for this discussion: the farmer-owned grain reserve and the recent payment-in-kind (PIK) program.

The PIK program grew out of the Reagan Administration's desperate search for a solution to an increasing agricultural surplus and plummeting farm prices and income in 1982. Federal budget outlays for farm price supports were rising as a result.

Taking land out of production, reducing supplies and thereby boosting prices are old methods of farm income support. The PIK program renewed this approach by offering farmers not cash, but government-owned surplus grain, in exchange for taking acreage out of production. Farmers could then sell the grain or hold it in hopes that prices would rise.

This program began early in 1983, and the response was enormous. A total of 82 million acres was enrolled, or a 36 percent reduction in planted acreage. Coupled with a severe drought in the summer of 1983, PIK cut sharply – too sharply – into both production and grain reserves.

PIK was rife with problems. First its cost: $9-$12 billion, depending on whose numbers are used. Secondly, much of the grain went to huge farmers who were not in economic difficulty. The single largest transfer of PIK wheat – $3.7 million worth – went to the J.G. Boswell Co., a mammoth corporate farm in California. The huge grain-trading multinationals reaped a windfall when PIK enrollment in some regions became so extensive that USDA did not have enough grain on hand to meet the demand and they had to sell or transport (or both) grain for use in the program. Finally, the program was supposed to require soil conservation methods on unplanted PIK acres, but on millions of acres farmers failed to do so.[16]

PIK helped bail out the Reagan Administration farm policy, but it is ironic that the stored grain that made PIK possible came out of a reserve set up under President

Carter.[17]

The idea of a grain reserve – of saving surplus food when the harvest is good against that inevitable day when the harvest is poor – is very old. The present farmer-owned grain reserve was part of the 1977 farm legislation. In periods of excess wheat production and declining prices, the reserve draws supplies off the market when prices are low. This in turn boosts prices and moderates some of the boom-and-bust nature of the agricultural economy.

The Reagan Administration does not approve of the reserve, although one might think that the disastrous overproduction and resultant enormous budgetary costs of the early 1980s would change a few minds. The reserve concept is foreign to the notion of an unfettered, free market agriculture – a goal most Republican farm policy makers have espoused.

Farm programs and farm size

A major problem with the commodity programs is that most of the benefits end up in the hands of the biggest farmers. In 1981, experts at USDA's Economic Research Service published a study on participation in the 1978 price programs for wheat, feed grains, cotton and rice. The study revealed that the largest 10 percent of the farmers participating – those with 500 acres or more – received 45.8 percent of the money. Farmers with less than 220 acres made up 72.1 percent of the participants, but received only 25.8 percent of the benefits. Very small operations – those with less than 70 acres – got 6.0 percent of the payments, but totaled 39.5 percent of the participants.[18]

The commodity programs have a payment limitation of $50,000, but this ceiling affects very few operators. The programs also have other problems:

● Benefits become capitalized into land values. The resultant higher values for real estate benefit farm owners, but more than a third of the acreage in commodity programs is rented. On those acres, price-support benefits enhance the position of landlords, even though the programs were originally created for farm operators.

● Supports have also led to artificially higher crop prices. This has meant that farmers produced more, using more land and other inputs, than market prices might otherwise have dictated.

● The programs have fueled the trend toward fewer and larger farms. As additional production, encouraged by the benefit programs, flowed into the markets, prices were further depressed. Farmers usually respond to price drops by expanding volume of production in order to keep up income. As we have seen, expansion leads to concentration as expanding farmers begin to eye the farm next door.

New directions

Commodity programs have, for the most part, failed in their appointed task of supporting farm income. The farm economy is still boom-and-bust. Needed urgently is more long-range planning and management for the sector. While this suggestion is heresy to many people involved in agriculture, there is really no other rational choice. The experience of the 1980s – particularly the extravagant and untargeted PIK program – demonstrates vividly that some change is needed.

One response is an old one: government should get out of agriculture. But what this means is not clear. Without the stability provided by public programs, the inherently unstable business of farming would probably return to the disastrous tendencies of the 1920s. Price swings would be even wider.

The nation needs policy that will flatten or reduce natural peaks and valleys. Also needed are steps to ensure that price-support mechanisms do not fuel economic concentration, are targeted toward small and moderate-size operations, and can be carried out at reasonable cost.

A few specific recommendations:

- The farmer-owned grain reserve should be retained and expanded.
- Policy should aim more toward supporting the incomes of small and mid-size farm operators, rather than supporting commodity prices.
- A payment limit of $20,000 per farmer should be imposed and enforced.
- Some form of mandatory production controls such as allotments should be established. Without such controls, the boom-and-bust cycle will never be broken.

Agricultural labor: the harvest of shame isn't over

Hired farmworkers, particularly migratory workers, remain at the bottom of our society. Despite some new protections and progress in the last two decades, farmworkers have household incomes that are about half the national average; are in poorer health; are more likely to suffer accidents; live in poorer-quality housing; have lower levels of education; and are much more likely to be under-employed than other Americans. In addition, farmworkers are exposed almost daily to toxic pesticides and herbicides.

In 1981, median earnings for hired farmworkers amounted to $2,841 for males and $1,465 for females. These are the lowest earnings figures in the Census Bureau's schedule of more than fifty occupational classifications.[19] But even these meager jobs are disappearing, as many farmworkers are displaced by increasing mechanization of production and harvests.

USDA's 1981 report on the structure of agriculture sums up the dilemma of the labor situation:

Labor is an important resource in agricultural production, the one that makes all the others work. Modern industrialized agriculture is increasingly looking to hired workers to meet its labor needs, yet the current farm labor market structure and environment is not satisfactorily meeting the needs of farm-workers, employers, or the larger society.

For many of the nearly three million people employed by farmers, the farm-labor market frequently fails to provide stable employment opportunities with reasonable levels of earnings and the working conditions they seek.

By virtually any objective economic measure, farmworkers as an occupational group fall below minimally acceptable labor-force standards. . . .

At the same time, many farm employers are having difficulty hiring adequate numbers of sufficiently productive workers to produce competitively in domestic and world markets.[20]

A conflict arises between two contradictory goals. Understandable public concern over the economic status, health and other problems of farmworkers clashes with a desire for inexpensive food. Most of the time cheap food comes out on top.

Farmers and their families do most of the work in U.S. agriculture, but the importance of hired labor is growing. As farms become fewer in number and larger in size, requirements for hired workers rise. Many farms have passed the point at which one family's labor is sufficient to complete the work.

Every year, at least three million persons are engaged in at least some hired farm work and about one in three farms uses hired labor. Larger operations and a few regions account for almost all this labor. More than one-third of all expenditures for farm labor are in California, Florida and Texas, and more than a third of these expenses come from the largest 2 percent of farms.[21]

There are several types of hired farm labor. Some of it is full-time, 'hired hand' kind of employment, some of it is seasonal and involves local people – often students or neighbors – who have other income sources, and some of it involves seasonal, migrant laborers who depend on farm work for their living. Discussions of 'farmworker' problems usually are about the people who fall into the last category. No one really knows how large the whole farm labor force is, nor how big the migratory farm labor force is. One observer has noted that the U.S. government knows more about migratory fowl than it does about migratory workers.

Part of the problem in estimating the size of the farm labor force is that a large percentage of the work force consists of illegal, undocumented workers. A 1980 USDA study placed the number of farmworkers at about three million. But other studies (notably one done for the Legal Services Corporation in 1977)[22] indicate that there are closer to five million farmworkers in the U.S. USDA studies indicate that the farm labor force is predominantly white, while other research compiled by the Farmworker Justice Fund shows that about 50 percent of the farm labor force is Hispanic and 30 percent is black.[23]

The danger of exposure to pesticides is probably the leading farm labor issue of the mid-1980s. A growing body of evidence on this issue shows that farmworkers often are exposed to toxic farm chemicals in violation of state and federal laws. Even when the laws are obeyed, exposure can be dangerous, in part because the long-term impact on health is not known. It is clear, however, that many pesticide poisonings of farmworkers involve much more than a headache of a few hours. Many workers are exposed not from direct handling of the chemicals, but from contact with fields and crops where spraying has occurred.

This problem is on the rise. For example, in 1964, the state of California recorded 1,347 work-related acute pesticide poisonings. By 1980 the figure was up to 1,741, but it is highly probable that these figures understate the problem. The incidence of occupational injury and illness has been increasing for agricultural workers while it has been declining in most other sectors:[24]

	Rates per thousand full-time employees		
	1975	1980	1981
Agriculture	10.5	11.9	12.3
Mining	11.0	11.2	11.6
Construction	15.9	15.7	15.1
Manufacturing	13.0	12.2	11.5
Private sector, total	9.1	8.7	8.3

New directions

A new policy for agricultural labor should have four facets:

● A federal labor relations act modelled after California's successful statute, which guaranteed collective bargaining rights to the state's farmworkers. Another way to reach a similar goal would be to apply the standards of all federal labor laws to agricultural employers and workers.

● A requirement that farmers comply with all federal labor laws to be eligible for participation in federal farm programs.

● An attempt by government to identify and disseminate ideas for better labor-management practices and relations in agriculture.

● Strengthening of federal and state pesticide safety regulations and licensing. This should include maintaining current standards and setting tougher requirements in some other areas.

A 1980 USDA report examined several large-farm operations that have adopted progressive labor techniques long used by non-farm businesses. These farms provided training to improve workers' skills in order to increase productivity and efficiency. In return, the farmworkers receive a better wage and benefit package. Workers are then much more likely to remain with the farm. Both sides benefit. Employers are pleased to have a more stable and productive work force, while employees are happy about their improved economic situation.

An example of this type of change is found in Coastal Growers, a California farm cooperative. In 1965, Coastal Growers hired a personnel professional to manage hired lemon pickers. The results have been excellent:

- Productivity increased from four boxes picked per hour in 1964 to eight and a half boxes by 1980.
- Wages increased 218 percent between 1965 and 1978, as contrasted to 139 percent for all farm laborers in California.
- Average employee's work period was extended from 17 to 89 days.[25]

Widespread adoption of this model would require several steps. Labor laws should be enforced to prevent under-cutting of such experiments by unscrupulous employers. Employers, workers and public officials all need education in the benefits of this approach. This could come in part through the Extension Service, the state-federal network of practical education for rural America. Training will be needed to develop a larger number of competent pro-fessionals with skills in modern farm labor personnel work. Farmworker groups and employers could contribute to this training process. Research by the Departments of Agricul-ture and Labor is also needed to identify the best models.

Farming the tax code: a bumper crop

Taxes are a final consideration in any business. In agriculture, the taxes must be paid after the crop has been sold. But today this logic is being reversed. For a growing number of investors, absentee landlords and others seeking to shelter income, taxes have become the first, or even sole, consideration for deciding whether or not to get into agriculture.

Many observers believe that the Internal Revenue Code has had a greater impact on agricultural structure than any other public policies. The tax code includes many special provisions for agriculture, many of them dating from an earlier period when policy-makers thought farmers were too uneducated to decipher the rules. Tax policy has been a major contributor to the decline of the small and medium-sized family farm. A 1982 USDA study concludes that the tax laws have –

- Helped inflate the prices of farmland.
- Accelerated the trend toward larger individual farms.
- Encouraged production of some commodities solely for their value as tax shelters, even though this increases overproduction.
- Granted tax breaks to capital investment while imposing taxes on labor.
- Stimulated farm incorporation by wealthy investors and upper-income farmers. This means their tax burden is lower than most average-size non-corporate family farm operators.
- Encouraged purchase of farmland as a means of reducing estate taxes through the special inheritance rules for agriculture.[26]

Agriculture has become a very attractive shelter for high-income individuals who want to reduce their tax liability. Accountants and tax lawyers are eternally vigilant when it comes to looking for tax shelters, and in agriculture they have found some of the very best. But in the process, as tax researcher Chuck Hassebrook of the Nebraska-based Center for Rural Affairs says, 'We've lowered profits in farming and granted a competitive advantage to larger farmers and outside investors.'[27]

These investors are not concerned about making a living strictly from the land and pay more for farmland than the small-scale operator can afford. The small-farm operator or the would-be entrant is outbid. The tax-motivated investor is also less concerned about overproduction or resource conservation than about maximization of tax-shelter benefits.

Tax breaks are used by the small and medium-size farmer, but the wealthy outside investor – a doctor, lawyer or dentist, rather than a giant corporation – can reduce tax liabilities below zero. That is, taxes due on non-farm income can be reduced substantially through use of the extra write-offs available in agriculture. If this 'farmer' has enough non-farm income, low profits and even losses before taxes can be converted into sizeable after-tax gains.

Interfaith Action for Economic Justice, a church-affiliated public interest group, points out that farmers on an individual basis have little choice but to use the available tax breaks. Without them, economic survival in agriculture often would be impossible. But the cumulative impact of the various tax advantages and the entrance of shelter-seeking investors are results most people would find undesirable: 'larger farms, inflated values for most farm assets, over-production of the most tax-favored commodities, inefficient use of resources, and deterioration of rural communities.'[28]

Present policy

Several parts of the tax code as it applies to income have an impact on agriculture:

● *Capital gains treatment.* Farm income in many instances is considered capital gains and is thus subject to a lower tax than is regular income. Only 40 percent of capital gains income is taxable.
● *Interest payments.* Farmers, like other people, such as homeowners and credit card holders, may deduct interest payments from income. But with farm interest payments so large, farming is an especially lucrative

source of such deductions.

- *Accelerated depreciation.* Farmers and other business taxpayers may depreciate their investments in buildings and equipment at a much faster rate than the expenses actually produce income or decline in value.
- *The investment tax credit.* This credit may be taken, along with accelerated depreciation, for breeding stock, special-use agricultural buildings and farm machinery.
- *Cash accounting.* This special rule for accounting procedures is granted to farmers but not to most other businesses, which must use accrual accounting. The cash rule means that farm production expenses may be deducted immediately, on this year's tax return, rather than being balanced against the income generated from production on next year's return.

A wily investor or tax advisor can use all these devices to put together an attractive package of shelters. But they are shelters available to any owner of farm assets. Such an owner might be a bona fide family operator residing on and managing a farm, or an absentee owner seeking only the tax benefits.

Tax treatment of estates also is very important to agriculture. Since 1976, farms have been assessed, for tax purposes, at their use value rather than market value. Use value is almost always lower, reflecting the fact that a farmer must pay more for land than it generates in income or that land might be more valuable for non-farm uses. These provisions are most beneficial to heirs of large estates. The special treatment often induces wealthy individuals to try to convert part of their estates into agricultural assets.

To check this tendency, rules require that heirs must hold the land for fifteen years after the decedent's death, and that the land must be farmed by the family for five of the eight years before and five of the eight years after death. This slows down the shelter seekers somewhat, but it also ties up land for long periods. The estate tax provisions increase the demand for land by making it attractive as a shelter, but the provisions also limit the supply of land by restricting its post-inheritance sale. Both these conditions cause higher land prices.

The rules also encourage the creation of a landed aristocracy. Farm families and farm heirs have incentives to hold on to property which might otherwise end up on the real-estate market, opening up an opportunity for new farmers. That leads us all the way back to the first topic in this chapter – entry. According to Interfaith Action,

● Estate and gift tax rules . . . also encourage wealthy investors to build farm estates and to qualify themselves for the special estate tax features. Estate tax rules, no less than income tax rules, encourage fewer, larger farms, absentee investor ownership, and farmland price inflation.[29]

New directions

What should be done? While the benefits of the tax code are potentially useful to the average farm operator, investors and tax-loss farmers have much more to gain. In fact, the advantages gained by the average farmer are far outweighed by the concentration, inflation, overproduction and other problems caused by the code as it is now used. Estate taxation rules should be rewritten to favor the small and moderate-size farm. USDA's report on agricultural structure suggests taxing 'farmland death transfers *very* progressively, without exception, once the amount of land involved is larger than an efficient family-sized farm.'[30] More generally, a sensible course would be to eliminate all special preferences for agriculture in the income tax rules. Although it might at first be a hardship for many small and moderate-scale operators, it would benefit them in the long run by eliminating shelters for wealthy investors. This change would cut into overproduction, help curb price inflation in the land market, and oust a principal source of unfair competition with the family farm.

In the middle: farmers and consumers in the marketplace

In examining food marketing, we look in two directions – back to the farmer and ahead to the consumer. Both are often losers in the complex marketing system, while the winnings – the profits – go to those big firms in the middle who buy from the farmer and sell to the consumer.

If farmers have been lucky with weather, pests and other potential problems, at the end of the growing season they have a crop ready for market. But, for the most part, agricultural producers have little or no control over how they are able to market their crops. Farmers on the average receive only about 40 cents from each dollar spent by consumers for food. Some receive more; many receive much less, especially the producers of commodities that are altered, refined and processed several times into a product that bears little resemblance to the raw commodity in the fields. That degree of refining – whether it is a frozen dinner entrée, a box of 'Hamburger Helper', or a tennis-ball can of Pringle's potato chips – is responsible for food manufacturing industry profits, and for higher consumer prices.

This situation reflects the fact that agriculture is rarely a direct supplier of food to the consumer. Instead farmers are now

the sources of raw materials for a food system dominated by processing, distribution and marketing. This concept of agricultural production as a source of raw materials diverges from the traditional concept of agriculture as the food producer and the processing and distribution stages as mere vehicles for delivering farm products to the final consumer. The difference between the two ways of viewing production and processing might be subtle. However, it bears directly on the question of who controls or will control agriculture. It is one basis of much of the current concern about the future of independent family farms.[31]

Farmers are often controlled by market contracts or vertical integration. Marketing contracts coordinate farm production; at the beginning of a season farmers enter into agreements to sell to a single processor or other crop purchaser. This provides some security but locks the farmer into a set price. Vertical integration means production, processing and marketing are all concentrated in one firm.

Table 9 shows how marketing contracts and vertical integration have increased in some crops and livestock

TABLE 9 *Selected commodities produced under contracts and vertical integration, 1960-80*

Commodity	Marketing contracts			Vertical integration		
	1960	*1970*	*1980*	*1960*	*1970*	*1980*
			%			
All crops	8.6	9.5	14.3	4.3	4.8	5.3
Food grains	1.0	2.0	8.0	0.3	0.5	0.5
Feed grains	0.1	0.1	7.0	0.4	0.5	0.5
Fresh vegetables	20.0	21.0	18.0	25.0	30.0	35.0
Processed vegetables	67.0	85.0	85.0	8.0	10.0	15.0
Potatoes	40.0	45.0	60.0	30.0	25.0	35.0
Citrus fruits	60.0	55.0	65.0	20.0	30.0	35.0
Other fruits and nuts	20.0	20.0	35.0	15.0	20.0	25.0
Sugarbeets	98.0	98.0	98.0	2.0	2.0	2.0
All livestock items	27.2	31.4	38.2	3.2	4.8	10.1
Fluid milk	95.0	95.0	95.0	3.0	3.0	3.0
Eggs	5.0	20.0	52.0	10.0	20.0	37.0
Broilers	93.0	90.0	89.0	5.0	7.0	10.0
Turkeys	30.0	42.0	62.0	4.0	12.0	28.0
All farm products	15.1	17.2	22.9	3.9	4.8	7.4

Source: David Harrington *et al.*, *U.S. Farming in the Early 1980s: Production and Financial Structure*, USDA, ERS, Ag. Econ. Rept. 504, September 1983, p. 6.

items. Many of the major food items in our diet have come increasingly under these coordinated arrangements. For some crops, such as processed vegetables and broilers, contracts have long been a dominant reality. But now contracting is even on the rise for food grains and feed grains, the two biggest sellers in agriculture. More alarming is the rise of vertical integration in such crops as fresh vegetables, fruits, eggs and turkeys. Under marketing contracts, the farmer at least retains some semblance of autonomy, although it may be very slight. But with vertical integration the owning-and-operating farmer disappears entirely.

A large part of the change in marketing trends has to do with technology. Changes in marketing technology and methods of procurement have mostly moved toward larger producers selling to larger food-processing buyers. Large farms may also be favored in such arrangements as vertical integration. These forces may help drive more small-scale farms out of business. Thus the small-farm operator faces both difficulty in finding markets and competition from the larger farm in marketing.

Many buyers, few sellers: impacts on the consumer

Once the food processors, distributors, manufacturers and retailers have bought from the farmers and prepared consumer products, they are ready to sell. But what do these operations involve, and what are their impacts? While there are many more consumers than farmers, their lack of control in the food system may be just as great. At both ends – production and consumption – a large group of relatively powerless economic actors must deal with a small and powerful group of 'middlemen.' As the food system has become industrialized, that middle sector of processing and selling has grown rapidly and has become more and more powerful.

The economic clout of the food industry has become

enormous. It has been driven by the conglomeration of industries into oligopolies (shared monopolies). Economist Willard Mueller of the University of Wisconsin points out that conglomeration has taken place in distinct historical periods. By 1904 some anti-trust actions were underway, but many sectors had already been recast into oligopolies. For example, between 1890 and 1904, the American Tobacco Company absorbed 150 other firms and came to dominate 90 percent of the tobacco market. In the 1920s, dairy and food-retailing firms merged, but with other dairy companies or retailers. Conglomeration, the activity of the late 1960s, involves mergers between many different types of companies. This is the path followed by many food manufacturers.[32]

Conglomeration gives a firm great economic power. For example, Continental Baking provides only 5 percent of International Telephone and Telegraph's sales. But ITT can use its vast economic resources to put pressure on smaller baking competitors.

Beer is a dramatic and sad example of increasing concentration in the food industries. In 1970 Philip Morris acquired the Miller Brewing Company, then the seventh largest U.S. brewer, with $198 million in sales. Philip Morris was (and is) a huge conglomerate with $1.5 billion in annual sales – a conglomerate willing to invest heavily in promoting a new product line. Philip Morris's next steps were to begin U.S. production of the German beer Löwenbräu and, most important, to acquire the Lite brand from a small brewery in 1973. Miller Lite was born and enormous investments made in advertising. Today the Lite ads – featuring throngs of former professional athletes – are among the most popular and widely recognized on television. The result? By 1980, Miller had moved up to number two in beer sales, with 21 percent of the market, behind Anheuser-Busch's 28 percent. Five of the six other top brewers all lost sales between 1975 and 1980.[33] The consumer, battered and cajoled with a barrage of advertising, is in reality faced with an ever narrower choice of beers. Is it any wonder that Europeans and other visitors to the U.S. remark on the even-handed mediocrity and blandness of our beer?

Food industry concentration has increased most in those areas with extensive advertising, and beer is not the only example. Television ads increase concentration most dramatically. Recently, researchers looked at advertising-to-sales ratios of the top four firms in eighty-five food and tobacco groups. Those firms spending less than 1 percent of their incomes on advertising lost, on average, 0.6 percent of their market share. Those spending over 3 percent of income on advertising increased their market share an average of 16 percent, and most of these firms spent considerably more than 3 percent of their incomes on advertising.[34]

Present policy

For consumers and most farmers, existing programs in the marketing area have been of little help. An example is the agricultural marketing-order programs. In 1982, $6 billion dollars worth of food fell under the control of 47 marketing-order programs.[35] Under this system, producers of certain fruits, nuts or vegetables in an area may vote to place themselves under marketing restrictions on product quality and size. This is done to control supply and, hence, increase price.

In some years, large amounts of food are left to rot in the fields for 'economic' reasons. Sending them into the market would cause prices to plummet. Market orders are obviously harmful to the interests of consumers and, in fact, do not help most farmers. At the very least, farmers could still receive similar levels of income in a different system that would be less wasteful and would not penalize consumers.

Present policy toward economic concentration in the food industry is weak. The Reagan Administration Justice

Department has cast a very friendly eye on mergers. Similarly the Federal Trade Commission has backed away from close scrutiny of the food industry. An example is the agency's retreat on breakfast cereals, with respect to controlling television advertising aimed at young children and possible 'shared monopoly' charges against cereal manufacturers.

New directions

Several bold new steps could help change the marketing situation for both farmers and consumers:

● The marketing order system should be scrapped in favor of a system of direct payments for fruit and vegetable farmers, linked to better planning and coordination of supply and demand. Farmers would be guaranteed a price, and if the market price fell below that price, the producer would receive a payment to make up the difference between the guaranteed level and the lower market return. Consumers would benefit from a lower market price.

● The federal government should sponsor programs to encourage farmer-to-consumer direct marketing. Direct sales at roadside stands, pick-your-own farms, and urban farmers market sites have proven extremely popular with both producers and consumers. The farmer gets a better price by selling directly to consumers; the consumer may get a better price and certainly gets fresher, higher quality food; and both sides benefit from face-to-face contact.

● State and local governments can also promote direct marketing. In fact, many states – for example, West Virginia, California, Massachusetts, New York and Texas – have developed successful direct-marketing programs. Several cities (Hartford, Connecticut, Washington, D.C., New York and Baltimore, for example) also support farmers markets.

- Several steps can be taken to address economic concentration in the food industry. First, some controls must be placed on food-product advertising. Some or all of the standards for tobacco ads might serve as a model. A second useful step would be to strengthen and enforce existing laws against conglomerate mergers. All large mergers should be banned unless they enhance competition. Third, Congress should enact a federal corporate-chartering law to replace the present system of state charters. A few states, particularly Delaware, are famous for their lax chartering requirements; not surprisingly, most multinational firms are Delaware corporations. A new federal chartering law should replace this piecemeal system with more exacting controls and reporting standards, requirements for public members of boards of directors, and other reforms.

3 Fire in the earth: Technology, resources and the environment

Agriculture harnesses natural processes – plant and animal growth – for the most practical of ends: food and fiber production. Even in its highly industrialized, modern form, agriculture remains a natural process, dependent upon the proper combination of plant nutrients, water and solar energy.

Since the beginnings of U.S. agriculture, an urgent and on-going need for food meant that the environmental consequences of food production were less important than human need. Resources were abundant and the task at hand was to fend off starvation; the emphasis was on maximum efficiency of production. But some agricultural practices, while effective in the short run, have created conditions that could, over a longer period, threaten sustained productivity. Each section in this chapter deals with a key input for agricultural production, and each is presented in terms of the major issue or controversy surrounding its use. These issues include:

- Soil erosion and other soil problems
- Water use and availability
- Agricultural land preservation
- Energy use and availability
- Use of farm chemicals
- Genetic conservation and monocultural production

Soil conservation: eroding the future

Soil erosion is one of the most ominous problems in the food system. The loss of topsoil through erosion is a natural process, unavoidable in agriculture and not alarming if kept under control. But modern intensive production has increased the rate of soil loss on the most fragile lands to intolerable levels. Erosion may be caused by water or wind, although water is the major cause. The major types of water-caused damage are sheet erosion (the washing off of a thin layer of soil) and rill erosion (the formation of small tracks or channels in the topsoil that allow soil to wash away).

Wind and water erosion remove about 6.5 billion tons of topsoil every year. Most of this occurs on cropland and rangeland, but the loss is not distributed evenly. Instead, most erosion occurs on relatively few acres. The average erosion rate per acre of cropland is 4.7 tons a year, a level just below the accepted tolerable rate of 5 tons per acre. But in 1977, 51.2 percent of the major erosion occurred on only 8.7 percent of the country's total cropland acreage – an erosion rate of 10 tons or more per acre. The loss is much higher on the most erodible acres. Wind erosion in the Texas-New Mexico High Plains averages between 20 and 50 tons per acre. Hilly cropland in the Palouse Basin of Washington and Idaho erodes at annual rates of 50 to 100 tons per acre. And in Iowa, cropland erodes at a rate of 10 tons per acre.[1]

Erosion rates also are higher for certain crops – 19.9 tons per acre each year for cotton, 12.6 tons for sorghum, 8.2 tons for soybeans, and 7.6 tons for corn. Production of one pound of corn erodes five to six pounds of topsoil.

Over a third of American cropland erodes at rates in excess of five tons per acre. In 200 years of American agriculture, the nation lost one-third of available topsoil, sometimes at a rate of an inch of soil every one or two decades. The soil will eventually regenerate itself, but that takes between 100 and 1,500 years, depending upon local conditions. At current rates, 25 percent more soil is eroding than during the Dust Bowl of the 1930s, even though less land is now under cultivation.

The cost of erosion is huge. Every inch of soil lost in the Corn Belt means a loss of three bushels of corn per acre. Annual erosion losses include 12 million tons of nitrogen fertilizers and 3 million tons of phosphorus, valuable nutrients worth $1.6 billion. Eroded soil winds up in streams, rivers and oceans. Removing this silt from waterways costs as much as $500 million annually, and the silt itself reduces reservoir capacities. In terms of soil productivity, erosion causes a loss equivalent to the removal of 1.7 million acres of land from agriculture each year.[2]

Between the New Deal and the early 1970s, large amounts of land were taken out of cultivation, both to help conserve soil and to reduce commodity surpluses. But after the big 1972 grain sale to the Soviet Union, millions of acres came back into production, drawn by the lure of higher crop prices, expanded export markets, and the exhortations of farm policy makers to plant fence-row-to-fence-row. Between 1969 and 1980 land in wheat increased by 27 million acres. Overall land in row crops increased by almost 50 million acres. However, the best cropland was already in production. Expansion of planted acreage took place on land most susceptible to erosion – fragile and best left in pasture or other less intensive uses. Expanded export markets have been touted as the answer to all of agriculture's economic problems. But more exports mean more production and increased erosion is one certain result. By the year 2000, it is estimated that 36 to 143 million acres of now uncultivated land may come into crop production because of rising demand, bringing with it severe soil loss problems.

Present policy

A number of policies and programs affect soil conservation at the federal, state and local levels. As with many other federal agriculture programs, extensive policy development began with the New Deal. Severe erosion during the Dust Bowl years culminated in 1934 when wind damage was so extensive that huge clouds of dust fell on the cities of the East Coast and even on ships several hundred miles out in the Atlantic.

These disastrous conditions led, in 1935, to the formation of the Soil Conservation Service (SCS) within the Department of Agriculture and, in 1936, to passage of the Soil Conservation and Domestic Allotment Act. The Act authorized the Agricultural Conservation Program (ACP). Still the principal soil conservation apparatus of the federal government, ACP provides cost-sharing to farmers for installation or use of conservation methods. The ACP budget in fiscal year 1984 was $190 million, and about $8 billion has gone into the program since 1936. Work under ACP funding has included construction of more than 2 million miles of terraces, strip-cropping of 115 million acres, and a number of other conservation activities.

The cost-sharing approach sounds effective, but it has not been. Much of the money has been spent on techniques oriented toward production rather than erosion control or on land that poses few erosion risks. A General Accounting Office report found that less than half the ACP dollars spent in 1976-77 went to conservation-oriented systems.[3]

Another major federal soil protection effort came in 1977 – the Soil and Water Resources Conservation Act. This law mandated a new system of evaluation and long-range planning for conservation. USDA was directed to establish both a framework for policy planning and an on-going inventory and appraisal of natural resources.

There also are soil conservation efforts at the state and local levels. Most prominent is the network of almost 3,000 local Soil Conservation Districts. The districts are not under federal control but use personnel of the Soil Conservation Service for technical assistance. The districts provide an effective system for implementation of conservation policies.[4]

Some states have their own programs. Iowa, for example, has a five-year plan recommending a number of specific actions, including a tillage program and incentives to control wind erosion. Other recommendations in the plan include an income tax credit for expenses of adopting permanent conservation technologies. Iowa also has a cost-sharing program, as do five other Midwestern states.[5]

New directions

A number of steps are needed, all of which should fit within a broad national policy for agricultural resource conservation and environmental protection. The soil portion of that policy should include:

- Regular analysis by USDA of the effectiveness of its soil programs.
- Targeting of the cost-sharing and technical assistance programs on land with the most severe erosion problems.
- Tougher standards for use of cost-sharing funds, to ensure support of conservation-oriented practices.
- Establishment of a conservation reserve which would pay farmers a small per-acre fee to take highly erodible land out of production.[6]

Water use and misuse

Water looms as the major agricultural resource crisis of the late twentieth century. Agriculture is a voracious user of water, mostly for irrigation. In 1980, irrigation accounted for 83 billion of the 100 billion gallons of fresh water consumed each day in the United States. And another 2 to 3 percent of that total went to livestock uses.[7] This level of consumption is remarkable enough in itself, although a distinction should be made between consumption and withdrawal (use) of water. Of the 1,260 billion gallons of water flowing daily into the nation's streams, 315 billion gallons are withdrawn. But most of this total is returned to the streams; only 96 billion gallons a day are consumed – agriculture accounts for most of that consumption.[8]

Irrigation has successfully turned millions of acres of arid land into productive farms, but it has also created many resource and environmental problems. While irrigation is the leading issue in farm water use, other problems exist, particularly pollution.

The number of irrigated acres has risen substantially since 1900:

Year	Millions of acres
1900	7.2
1930	14.6
1945	20.7
1955	30.0
1975	45.3
1978	51.3

Along with the development of water for other uses, irrigation has been the foundation for tremendous economic growth of some areas, particularly the West and Southwest. Irrigated land in central and southern California, once a desert, now produces a very large part of the nation's output of fruits, vegetables, cotton, and other crops. Since the Second World War, the spread of irrigation has been particularly rapid. Expansion was especially dramatic in a few states.[9] (See table below.)

More recently, irrigation has even spread to the Eastern areas of the country. For example, between 1974 to 1978, irrigated acreage east of the Great Plains increased by 65 percent.

| | *Thousands of irrigated acres* | |
	1939	1974
California	4,277	7,749
Kansas	83	2,010
Nebraska	474	3,967
Texas	895	6,594

Irrigation has created three major problems: depletion of water resources, salinization and land subsidence. Depletion is the most obvious problem. Fresh water supplies are found either on the surface of the earth, in rivers, streams and lakes, or beneath the surface, in ground water reservoirs. These surface water supplies are being heavily used. Urban development and energy production in the Western states will place heavy demands on surface water reserves already stretched thin.

Ground water supplies are being used even more quickly than supplies in rivers and streams. More than 97 percent of fresh water supplies in the U.S. are underground, and ground water makes up about 70 percent of the water used for irrigation in the seventeen Western states. Once surface water supplies met most irrigation needs, but today ground water is the major source. Use of ground water for all purposes has increased from 35 billion gallons a day in 1950 to 90 billion gallons a day in 1980.

Irrigation is rapidly depleting ground water resources in some areas. The most notable example is the Ogallala aquifer, a huge underground reservoir reaching from Nebraska to Northwestern Texas. Once 150,000 square miles of land atop the aquifer could be used only for grazing or dry land farming, if at all. Irrigation changed all of this drastically, making such areas as the Texas High Plains productive centers for cotton and other crops. But Ogallala water is being pumped out much faster than it can be replenished through rainfall. Some irrigated Texas farms have already been forced back into dry land production.

It is rapidly becoming very expensive to get the water out

of the ground and onto the crops. This pumping process requires energy to fuel irrigation pumps, and the resulting cost is passing the break-even point. A 1980 USDA study predicts that if natural gas prices continue to rise, irrigation of major crops in a thirty-two-county area of the Texas High Plains will end by 1995. Annual net income from crop production in that area would decline from $277 million to $164 million.[10]

Salinization occurs when land is inundated with more water than natural drainage can remove. The soil becomes waterlogged, and the water dissolves soil salts which then rise to the surface in concentrated form. This hinders crop growth and eventually destroys the land's productivity. Salinization has cut productivity by 25 to 35 percent on irrigated crop land in the United States. The problem is severe in California's San Joaquin and Imperial Valleys. In the San Joaquin, some 400,000 acres suffer reduced productivity; and it is projected that this acreage could rise to 700,000 by the year 2000 if the problem is not checked. This would mean an annual productivity loss of $321 million.[11]

The particular problem in the San Joaquin Valley is accumulation of saline water beneath the surface of the land. This retards growth by affecting a plant's roots. Washing out salts concentrated on the surface moves the problem a few inches underground, but does not eliminate it. One solution to salinization is construction of underground drainage systems, but this is a slow and expensive process.

Subsidence occurs when the land surface sinks as a result of intensive irrigation, mining or oil drilling. When the water or minerals helping support the surface of the land are withdrawn, a collapse is likely. Irrigation is a major cause. In the irrigated San Jacinto Valley of California, subsidence has been occurring at a rate of 1.2 feet per year over an area of 5,400 square miles of crop land.[12] Subsidence is usually a permanent change in the condition of the land and limits agricultural uses.

Water pollution also is an important issue. It arises from a number of sources – urban, industrial and agricultural. Farming activities can cause water pollution from point sources, such as feedlots, and from non-point sources, such as runoff and fertilizer seepage. Non-point pollution has become a serious cause of nitrate contamination of water supplies.

Present policy

Most water law is a matter of state jurisdiction, and as water-use policy now exists in most states, there is little incentive for conservation. Federal policies have subsidized irrigation to such an extent that very cheap water has been made available. As of 1975, $16.9 billion had been invested in the development of irrigation for agriculture. Of this total, $9 billion came from federal sources, with the rest from other public and private financing. This averages out to a capital investment of $375 for each irrigated acre.

New directions

Clearly the old era of growth in irrigated agriculture and unlimited access to water is coming to an end. Economic growth and energy development in the West mean new competition for scarce water supplies. Agriculture probably will be incapable of competing with these more heavily capitalized uses. Growing concern with pollution will also lead to changes in the way agriculture uses water.

Depletion and cost mean that future irrigation will continue only on a much-reduced scale. Policy should help develop conserving technologies. Many such technologies are known: canals can be lined to move water less wastefully; sprinklers are less wasteful than flooding an entire field; and drip irrigation directs water through tubes to individual plant-root systems. Research is also proceeding on development of drought-resistant plants.

Major changes are needed in state water laws. Some important changes are underway or are being tested, but water law must move away from a premise of abundance to one of scarcity. Current policy – or its absence – allows and even encourages rapid withdrawal of water resources. For example, with no restrictions on withdrawals farmers who do not pump out ground water rapidly find their irrigating neighbors draining supplies.

In 1980 Arizona started a new ground water use program. Farmers now are faced with limits on the right to pump, pumping taxes, and declining future amounts of available water. These restrictions may seem harsh, but the new law which instituted the reforms also states that agriculture will remain a priority user.[13] Given the political and economic competition for access to water supplies, the farm community might well be advised to accept this compromise.

Water pollution could be checked in two ways. Reduced use of farm chemicals would mean less non-point contamination. Smaller livestock feedlots would mean less point-source water pollution.

Paving it over: the loss of agricultural land

You can see it from the freeway, from an airplane, in the suburbs, on a drive near almost any urban area and in many thoroughly rural areas – the spread of urban development, industry, shopping centers, mining and other activities which convert agricultural real estate to non-agricultural uses.

Conversion of farmland results from many causes. The supply of land is finite, but the uses demanded of that fixed number of acres are growing constantly. As the nation's population has grown, as millions have left the country and moved to the cities, as the demand for housing has increased, and as transportation networks have spread, new demands have fallen on the nation's land base. Since 1970 rural population growth has exceeded urban population growth. Seeking a better style of life, many people have chosen to escape the cities. But this is not a return to agriculture; it is more often city people wanting to own ten acres in the country. This means new pressure on agricultural land as the migrants buy up available sites.

Some experts believe the loss of farmland– particularly prime agricultural land – has reached crisis proportions. Others contend that, while we are losing productive farmland, the rate of conversion is not enough to cause alarm. But whatever its magnitude, there is a problem. Even if the conversion level is relatively low, much of the loss occurs near population centers where continued food production is highly desirable and where land is often the best.

Between 1967 and 1975, about 23 million acres of agricultural land moved into other use categories. This averages out to an annual loss of nearly three million acres. But this loss is not three million planted acres of corn and soybeans. As the 1980 National Agricultural Lands Study noted:

> of the average annual conversion of three million acres, 675,000 acres were from cropland; 537,000 were from range and pasture; 825,000 were from forest land; and 875,000 acres were from other land uses.[14]

The total amount of land in the United States is approximately 2,264 million acres. Of this aggregate figure, 465 million acres are cropland, and 221 million of the 465 million are in soil classes I and II, the best land. A loss of 675,000 acres means that about 0.15 percent of the cropland base is converted each year. This does not appear to be a serious problem, yet rising demand for food, worsening soil erosion, increasing constraints on energy resources, and an array of other problems may mean that some day we will need every available acre.

The best sites for agriculture – flat, well-watered land –

are also ideal for the construction of cities, towns and suburbs. In fact, 17 percent of U.S. farms actually are within Standard Metropolitan Statistical Areas (SMSAs). (The term was changed to Metropolitan Statistical Areas [MSAs] in 1983.) In 1974, those farms produced 24 percent of all commodities sold in the U.S. and 63 percent of the specialty crops. In the Northeast 46 percent, and in the Pacific states 56 percent of all commodities sold, were produced in counties within SMSAs.[15] Agriculture near cities is very important; loss of prime farmland means that food production will move farther and farther away from consumers.

Present policy

Land use regulation is primarily a state and local matter, and it is at those levels that most governmental attempts have been made to curb farmland loss, although the federal government has become involved to some extent.

Several preservation methods have been used at the state and local levels with varying degrees of success. Forty-eight of the fifty states have at least one preservation program, but no single effort can really withstand the pressure to convert. This is not to suggest that conversion is always a negative. It must be balanced against the demand for new housing and other needs. An appropriate middle-ground should be sought, satisfying as many interests as possible.

The most widely used preservation method is property tax assessment of farmland at its value for agricultural purposes, rather than for some more lucrative use. In 1956 Maryland enacted a preferential assessment law that was the nation's first farmland preservation program. All but two states now have some form of preferential assessment. In some of these laws tax relief is not accompanied by any obligation on the part of the farmer. But in the more effective statutes, participating landowners must agree to keep their farms in agriculture for a certain period in exchange for the tax break. Some state laws require repayment of the taxes saved, plus a penalty, if preferentially assessed land is shifted to other uses within a set span of years. But even penalties have failed to halt conversion because the profits made from sale of commercially valuable land generally exceed any penalty or tax roll-back. A 1976 Council on Environmental Quality study found that preferential assessment laws generally have been ineffective.[16]

Creation of agricultural districts is another state approach: the state designates certain areas for farming on a long-term basis. New York, with a program dating from 1971, is the pioneer in this area. Farms within a district are eligible for property tax relief and are to some extent protected from government condemnation for expansion of public services. Districting, like preferential assessment, has not been an effective shield against development.

A third preservation method involves purchasing from farmers their right to future development of land. Called purchase of development rights (PDR), this idea has been adopted in a few states and counties, notably New Jersey, Maryland and Suffolk County, New York. In these programs, the state or county pays the farmer the difference between the value of land for agriculture and its value for other, so-called 'higher' uses. This difference is the value of the development rights. In return, the farmer contracts to keep the land in agriculture permanently. PDR schemes can be quite effective since the land is legally bound to remain in farming even if sold. The stumbling-block is money – even a partial PDR program can be enormously expensive.

Zoning is an effective, but politically controversial, method of preservation. Among the states, only Hawaii has a state-wide zoning plan for agriculture, and Oregon requires local farm-use zoning and planning based on state standards. In addition, according to the National Agricultural Lands Study, some 270 counties and municipalities have enacted agricultural zoning ordinances or plans.

Zoning can be a very useful tool, but it suffers from several major limitations:

● Economic and political opposition will normally preclude passage of a tough zoning law.
● Even a moderately rigorous plan is subject to change if the political winds shift.
● Most local government zoning schemes use a minimum lot size approach, e.g., ten acres. This prevents a housing development of quarter- or half-acre lots, but, as the National Agricultural Lands Study noted, in practice the minimum lot size defines a farm. This process can result in the chopping-up of good agricultural land into these minimum-sized lots.[17]

Transfer of development rights (TDR) has been used by a few counties and municipalities. In a TDR program, the local planning agency or governing body designates both preservation and development zones. Land in preservation zones may not be converted. Land in development zones may be put to more intensive uses, but only after a would-be builder has purchased development rights from landowners in preservation zones. These rights are assigned to the preservation zone owners by the planning agency. In essence, TDR makes developers pay for the loss of preservation zone owners' right to convert their land.

The federal government has relatively little clout in this area, and usually exhibits less inclination to act. Federal estate-tax laws, as discussed in Chapter 2, have, since 1976, allowed farms to be assessed at their use value rather than their full market value. Most prominent among federal actions was the National Agricultural Lands Study (NALS), a two-year effort chaired by USDA and the Council on Environmental Quality, which included ten other departments and agencies. The NALS project conducted an extensive survey of the problem and made recommendations for preservation.

Unfortunately, federal policy has done more to contribute to farmland loss than it has to solve the problem. For example, NALS catalogued ninety different federal programs that contribute to farmland loss. Examples include programs for housing construction, highways, the building of reservoirs, and other purposes.

In summary, present efforts to curb the problem appear ineffective. Despite rhetoric about loss of agricultural land and many statutes and programs, the problem remains. Many farmers may be helped economically by programs such as preferential tax assessment, but the impact on farmland conversion is slight.

New directions

Local and state governments must combine a variety of methods into an overall package. An agricultural districting and preferential assessment program could be combined with mandatory farm-use zoning. A transfer of development rights program could be set up, and for a limited number of farms in selected areas a small purchase of development rights program would be useful.

Oregon may have the best statewide preservation program. The centerpiece is a requirement that all counties establish agricultural zoning plans that conform to specified statewide goals. All land in the top farm soil classes and currently devoted to agriculture must be zoned exclusively for farming. Municipalities create specific limits and engage in no more annexation outside those boundaries. A districting-like approach dictates that land in farm-use zones is exempt from special utility-tax levies and is eligible for preferential assessment and state inheritance tax breaks. This assortment of strategies is a sound approach for state and local governments.

Environmentalists Wendell Fletcher and Charles Little, writing for the *American Land Forum*, have taken a creative look at what states might do. They suggest the creation of 'farmland conservancies' and conservancy districts:

a local organization operating with a conservancy district coterminous with county or multi-county lines. The conservancy is empowered by state law to buy and sell land or rights in land for the purpose of maintaining prime . . . farm land in farm use; to use its lands to retain or increase the numbers of farms in appropriately-sized family proprietorships, and . . . to undertake needed soil and water conservation projects.[18]

Burning it up: energy use in the food system

The food system – production, processing, marketing, and home consumption – uses 16.5 percent of the energy consumed in the United States each year. Three percent of total energy is consumed by agricultural production. These numbers are not remarkable until some of the facts behind them are revealed.

Agriculture and the food system as a whole have become very closely linked to an extensive dependence on energy and energy-based products. Modern farms – with their large machinery, heating and drying needs, pesticides and fertilizers, irrigation systems, and other energy-using technologies – are highly vulnerable both to shortages of energy and to increases in its price. Similarly, the post-harvest marketing system relies on long-distance transportation, complex processing and packaging, and other energy-intensive systems.

Sudden embargoes or shortages might leave agricultural producers without access to essential fuels. Since farmers have difficulty passing higher costs on to those who buy raw agricultural products, any energy price increases, short- or long-term, will put pressure on net farm income. Higher energy input costs come out of the farmers' pocket.

Table 10 shows how production expenditures for energy and energy-related items have risen between 1940 and 1982. In 1940 the five items in the table made up 15 percent of total farm production expenses. But by 1982 this proportion rose to 22 percent. The share of the first four items – fertilizer, fuel, pesticides and electricity – grew from 11 percent of total expenses in 1940 to 18 percent in 1982.

This rapid increase in energy use is tied closely to the increasing capital intensity of agriculture and to the decline in farm numbers. Fewer people now work in agriculture, yet yields are higher. As has been noted earlier, the number of farms declined from well over six million in 1930 to 2.4 million in 1981. In 1910, 22.5 billion hours of human labor went into farm work every year. This figure stayed high until after World War II and then declined to only about 4.4 billion working hours in 1978. Capital has replaced labor, and a large part of the new capital has gone into either energy or technologies which consume energy.

Until 1973, fuels and power were abundant and relatively inexpensive for the food system and for other sectors of the economy. This is no longer the case, although energy input use is still high and continues to rise. Table 10 shows that, while total production expenses for agriculture rose twenty times between 1940 and 1982, expenses for energy inputs

TABLE 10 *Selected farm production expenses, 1940-82*

Year	Fertilizer and lime	Petroleum fuel and oils	Pesticides	Electricity	Repair and operation of motor vehicles and machinery	Total production expenses*
			Million dollars			
1940	306	350	44	28	306	6,664
1950	975	1,192	179	71	1,143	19,287
1960	1,344	1,484	290	177	1,742	26,599
1970	2,435	1,711	960	304	1,910	42,930
1975	6,660	3,318	1,783	594	3,417	72,849
1980	9,922	7,876	3,310	1,760	6,286	123,892
1981	10,074	9,109	3,569	1,975	6,369	131,819
1982	9,024	8,817	3,648	2,103	6,550	134,533

*Excluding dwellings of farm operators.
Source: USDA, ERS, *Economic Indicators of the Farm Sector: Income and Balance Sheet Statistics, 1982*, ECIFS 2-2, October 1983, pp. 70-2, 74.

rose even faster: nearly thirty times for fertilizer, twenty-five times for petroleum fuels, eighty-three times for pesticides, and seventy-five times for electricity.

Consider several details about energy use in food production:

- In 1981, crop production in the U.S. used on average about $4 worth of petroleum products per acre. Vegetable production cost $12 per acre.[19]
- More energy is used to produce synthetic fertilizers than goes into plowing, planting, cultivating and harvesting all U.S. crops. Production of one ton of ammonia requires 38,000 cubic feet of natural gas.[20]
- Farm use and costs of electricity have risen sharply. In 1965, farms in the U.S. had average monthly electricity bills of $16.30. By 1975, bills averaged $35.30 per month. But by 1981, the monthly average had jumped to $69.80. Higher rates are part of the reason for this jump, but amount of power used per farm also is up – from 716 kilowatt hours monthly in 1965 to 1,307 kilowatt hours in 1981.[21]
- As noted earlier in this chapter, the energy costs of irrigation pumping have risen steeply. These costs almost doubled between 1974 and 1977, rising from $570 million to $1,041 billion. Energy costs for certain irrigation systems went up even more in that three-year period. For example, natural gas costs per acre of corn produced by center pivot irrigation systems in the Oklahoma Panhandle were $9.45 in 1974 and $28.40 in 1977.[22]

Specific facts about energy-intensive food processing and marketing are just as startling:

- Processing uses one-third of the energy consumed by the total food system.
- Of the nation's total energy budget, 1.3 percent is used by food packaging. It takes 1,643 calories of energy to

produce a twelve-ounce can of soda containing 150
calories of food energy.

● Food travels long distances before it is consumed.
Trucks, which are more energy-intensive than rail
transport, are used to move 88 percent of all fresh
fruits and vegetables, and 99 percent of all livestock.[23]

Given this extensive dependence of the food system on
an increasingly expensive and potentially unreliable supply
of energy, policy should aim to conserve existing supplies
and to develop alternative sources. The problem is
complicated by the system's inefficient use of energy. Per-
acre yields have risen as mechanical and energy inputs have
replaced labor, but the rate of gain appears to have leveled
off in recent years. The era of ever-increasing productivity
as a result of new technology and greater use of inputs has
come to an end.

Even at the peak of this period, productivity rose at only
a fraction of the rate of increase in energy use. For
example, since 1945 use of machinery, liquid fuels, nitrogen
fertilizer, drying and electricity has increased substantially
in corn production. As a result, between 1945 and 1970 corn
yields per acre went up 135 percent, but use per acre of
various energy inputs increased as follows:[24]

	Percent increase
Electricity	870
Energy for drying	1,100
Gasoline	47
Insecticides	1,000 (1950–73)
Machinery	133
Nitrogen	1,500
Potassium	1,100

U.S. agricultural practices consume more energy than do
systems in most of the rest of the world. If energy-intensive
production technologies were used to feed all the earth's
population a U.S.-style diet, usable world petroleum
reserves would be exhausted in only thirteen years.[25]

Present policy

With a few notable exceptions, policy-makers have paid little attention to the real energy problems in food and agriculture. Government has subsidized irrigation, helped develop ever larger farm machinery, supported breeding of seeds and plants that require huge energy inputs, and generally promoted technology and energy use in agriculture. Conservation and alternative energy sources have been ignored for the most part. Farm policy has encouraged and promoted the substitution of capital for labor; the new capital has generally gone toward the purchase of fertilizer, pesticides, fuel and other energy-used products.

Some members of Congress have shown interest in energy alternatives for agriculture, but a similar focus at the Department of Agriculture has been much less evident. For the most part, the policy focus until the 1970s was on developing and promoting technologies capable of using an apparently endless supply of energy. In the new era of higher prices and reduced supplies, food-policy-makers are interested in securing or retaining access to energy stocks. Conservation is a rhetorical goal, but in 1982 USDA fired its only full-time specialist in organic farming, an approach to agriculture production based on conservation of energy and resources.

New directions

Two avenues offer a solution for agricultural energy problems. One is on-farm energy conservation and the other involves farm-based energy production for use both on and off the farm. The two are interrelated. While vulnerable to energy constraints, farmers also have the ability to solve some of their own problems, to conserve energy, and even to produce a portion of the energy needed on their farms.

Many farmers have already adopted various conservation

methods, including minimum tillage, better insulation of homes and farm buildings, regular maintenance of farm machinery and equipment, proper pairing of tractors and implements by size, and improved irrigation practices.

Energy also could be conserved through more widespread use of organic farming techniques. Almost one-third of the total energy input into agricultural production is used to make natural-gas-based synthetic nitrogen fertilizer. Replacing synthetic nitrogen partially or wholly with organic fertilizers – that is, with applications of animal manure and rotations of nitrogen-fixing plants – can reduce farm energy use. Organic methods could reduce the energy consumption of corn production by about 25 percent, for example. A 1976 National Science Foundation-funded study comparing organic and conventional farms found that the former achieved significant energy advantages not enjoyed by the latter.[26] And a 1980 USDA report concluded that organic farmers use appreciably less total energy than do conventional farmers.[27]

Agricultural production of energy – as distinguished from conservation – also offers some significant opportunities. Solar energy is one example. Solar technologies, for water heating, space heating, grain drying and other tasks are now available, but can be expensive to install. One way around this dilemma is to have farmers build and maintain their own solar systems. For example, working with the non-profit Small Farm Energy Project in Cedar County, Nebraska, cooperating farmers have installed a variety of home-built, inexpensive technologies that pay for themselves in just a few years.

Production of fuels using agricultural feedstocks is another possible solution. The best-known and most widely debated alternative in this arena is production of alcohol fuel – particularly as an additive for gasoline. Since the mid-1970s, there has been considerable interest in alcohol generation from such crops as corn and sugar. Farmers are attracted to 'gasohol' because of its potential as a market for crops. Energy conservationists are, of course, intrigued because of the possibility of reducing dependence on petroleum-based fuels. The federal government has undertaken a considerable amount of research and demonstration into alcohol fuels. Brazil has an even larger program, producing 1.3 billion gallons in 1980 for use in gasohol.

Alcohol fuels production sounds like a panacea, but it is not without problems. Sometimes more energy goes into the distillation process than is gained in the energy value of alcohol. In addition, large-scale production of alcohol for fuel might put stress on land resources and could divert some crops away from use as food. Potentially more useful are smaller-scale, on-farm production and use of alcohol. Also of great potential is the use of non-food feedstocks to produce alternative fuels. Methane gas production from animal and human wastes is an example.

Both energy conservation and alternative-fuel production need more government assistance and guidance. Specifically:

● Agricultural research and extension programs should include more emphasis on energy-saving and producing technologies useful to small and moderate-size farm operators.
● Public lending programs for farming should support development of these technologies.
● Much more research and extension work should be devoted to organic agriculture.

Out on a genetic limb: crop monoculture

A major contributor to the great leaps forward in agricultural productivity is the development of improved plant varieties. Scientific plant breeding has produced the seeds of the Green Revolution – plants capable of extremely high yields when used in conjunction with fertilizers, pesticides and irrigation systems. This improvement in plant varieties is but one of the latest chapters in a long history. Since the beginning of agriculture, farmers have cultivated the plants that would produce best. Moving away from naturally occurring plant varieties and complex ecosystems, farmers have created simpler ecosystems that require a great deal of careful cultivation.

This trend is called monoculture – the reliance on a single plant variety, or relatively few of them. Monoculture is the foundation of our modern ability to produce vast amounts of food, but it is also a potentially dangerous course. Putting all a farm system's productive eggs in one basket means that a single pest or weather change could wipe out most of the crop. This increasing genetic uniformity and resulting agricultural vulnerability have in fact been the cause of major crop failures throughout history. In Ireland in the 1840s, potato production was based on only a few plant varieties. A fungus destroyed half the crop in 1846, caused widespread hunger and starvation, and contributed to the mass migration of the Irish people. This situation is not remote history. A corn leaf blight in 1970 trimmed 15 percent (700 million bushels) off the U.S. corn crop and caused widespread concern.

A 1972 National Academy of Sciences study, responding in part to the corn blight, reported that the nation's genetic resource base is becoming perilously narrow.[28] Other researchers have come to similar conclusions. About 95 percent of the food consumed in the U.S. comes from only 30 crops. Six types of corn make up 71 percent of plant acreage, and two varieties of peas account for 96 percent of that crop's acreage.[29] This contrasts sharply with early agriculture, when hundreds of species were cultivated.

Shifting to reliance on a smaller number of more productive varieties is inevitable for a modern, industrial society. As a leading expert on these issues puts it:

> Monoculture is a feature of modern agriculture, and we shall have to learn to live with it. . . . The question is not whether we shall grow crops in pure stands over large areas; the question is how we can raise the crops on a large scale at minimum risk.[30]

Minimizing the risk means assuring that plant breeders and farmers retain the flexibility to shift to other varieties and develop strains resistant to new diseases, pests or conditions. This means adequate seed storage programs and banks. It is ironic that the major foods crops which now support the industrialized countries originated in the Third World. Examples include corn in Latin America, soybeans in China, and rice in India. The United States is the original home only of sunflowers, blueberries, cranberries, and Jerusalem artichokes. No crops originated in Northern Europe. Keeping viable both the many wild varieties and the variegated crop systems of the Third World is crucial for the future work of plant breeders. Yet the narrow uniform varieties, developed in wealthy countries as Green Revolution miracle seeds, have begun to spread to the old centers of diversity in Asia, Africa and the Middle East. In those regions, broad-based gene pools are being edged out of existence.

Also critical is the rise of corporate control of the seed industry. Economic power over seeds is concentrated in companies that also have sizeable interests in chemicals and energy. Four companies control two-thirds of all seed corn sales in the U.S. These and other big firms with interests in seeds want more legal and economic control, particularly in the form of plant patenting laws. These laws can lead to higher seed prices, corporate takeovers of seed companies, and the eventual loss of traditional seed varieties.

Present policy

Policy in this area has for the most part been directed at *achieving* a monocultural food production system, rather than at any concern about the consequences of that achievement. That was in fact the goal of agriculture from its earliest stages and remains so today. The challenge is to temper and control this trend so as to lessen the vulnerability of the whole system.

Three related areas of present federal activity are important – research, germplasm storage and plant patenting. Plant breeding research has been a concern of agricultural policy since the nineteenth century, but seed conservation and storage are more recent developments. The National Seed Storage Laboratory at Fort Collins, Colarado, dates from 1958 and was the first national cold storage facility for germplasm.

Plant patenting is an even more recent development, dating in the U.S. from the adoption of the Plant Variety Protection Act in 1970. This law shelters seed profits and has increased business competition for control of genetic resources.

New directions

In each of the three policy areas cited above, improvements are possible:

- Publicly supported research should include more emphasis on breeding of plants to help reduce dependency on monoculture. Researchers should pursue varieties that are less dependent on high levels of energy and chemical inputs. The predisposition to seek uniformity should give way to an effort to generate as much diversity as possible.
- Germplasm storage efforts need substantial improvement. Seed banks are essential for preservation of the genetic material needed by plant breeders. But in 1982, there were only thirty-three facilities worldwide for the long-term storage of seeds. The U.S. seed bank in Colorado is generally considered to be inadequate, with only 1,300 varieties in storage. That facility needs upgrading and increased funding.

The chemical fix

Agriculture in the last three to four decades has become heavily dependent on regular, large doses of chemical fertilizers, insecticides and herbicides. In addition, chemical additives are widely used in food manufacturing and marketing. These inputs have been major contributors to increased agricultural productivity, which has been viewed as the most important goal of the food system.

As Table 10 on page 79 indicates, pesticide and fertilizer use have increased dramatically over the past four decades. Between 1940 and 1982, farm production expenditures rose 2,850 percent for fertilizer and lime, and 8,190 percent for pesticides. Despite the constraints imposed by rising energy costs after 1973, use of chemicals has continued to rise. Commercial fertilizer consumption totaled 31.8 million tons in 1965, but rose to 53.3 million tons by 1981:

Million tons of commercial fertilizers consumed, U.S.[31]

1965	31.8
1970	39.6
1974	47.1
1975	42.5
1976	49.2
1977	51.6
1978	47.5
1979	51.5
1980	52.7
1981	53.3

The primary components of commercial fertilizer are nitrogen, phosphorus and potassium. In 1981, 11.8 million tons of nitrogen, 5.4 million tons of phosphorus and 6.2 million tons of potassium were used.[32] Chemical fertilizers are used on all the vegetables produced in the U.S., and on 96 percent of the corn, 77 percent of the cotton, and 62 percent of the wheat. On an average, U.S. agriculture uses 111 pounds of synthetic fertilizer and two pounds of pesticides for each acre of croplands.[33]

Half of all food marketed in this country has detectable levels of pesticide. Each year some half a million people in the world are poisoned by pesticides, including 45,000 in the U.S.[34] Pesticides and food additives are viewed as a threat to consumers, but it is becoming increasingly apparent that current agricultural practices are also harmful to the health of farmers and farmworkers.

A growing body of research links adverse health consequences with agricultural practices. For example, a University of Iowa study found that white male farmers in Iowa faced a uniformly greater threat from cancer than non-farmers. Of a number of types of malignancies, the study found that between 1971 and 1978 only lung cancer caused a higher mortality rate among non-farmers than among farmers.[35]

These data appear to contradict our cherished notion of farm life as healthy, clean and invigorating. The country has always been a mythical place of escape from the unhealthy cities, but it seems that conditions and practices in agriculture may be as dangerous as employment in an industrial plant.

The evidence indicates that exposure to pesticides is not the only problem. Health is also affected adversely by seepage of fertilizer into drinking water supplies. Application of large amounts of fertilizer can cause both nitrate contamination of water and eutrophication (reduction of oxygen in the water). Non-point farm sources account for more than 70 percent of the nitrogen which enters surface waters. Nitrate contamination of ground water is mainly a problem in agricultural areas, but the prospects for reducing fertilizer applications are bleak.

The 1980 *Global 2000 Report* projects that fertilizer use in the U.S. by the year 2000 will be 2.5 times as great as the level of consumption in the early 1970s and eight times as much as in the early 1950s. Even careful application of this greatly increased volume may lead to water pollution, atmospheric damage and soil deterioration. The National

Academy of Sciences says that nitrous oxide given off by fertilizer interaction with the soil can damage the ozone layer of the atmosphere. Higher levels of dangerous ultraviolet radiation would then reach the earth.[36]

Reliance on chemicals is reducing U.S. mineral stores and increasing dependence on imports. In 1979-80, the U.S. imported 19 percent of its nitrogen requirements. This compares to a period of self-sufficiency before 1974 when the U.S. was a net exporter of nitrogen. The U.S. is the world's leading producer of phosphate rock, but projections are that this dominance will decline after 1985 and that supplies will be exhausted by the year 2000. With regard to potash, the U.S. produced less than 25 percent of its requirements in 1979-80 and will produce less than 10 percent of its needs by 2000.[37]

Overuse makes very little sense in light of the fact that the chemicals are becoming increasingly less effective. In many instances, they are even counterproductive. For example, pests often develop a resistance to pesticides. In California, resistance to at least one type of pesticide has appeared in seventeen of twenty-five major agricultural pests. In addition, pesticides kill natural enemies of the pests.[38] Fertilizers also have become marginally less and less effective; they add to productivity, but in increasingly smaller increments.

Present policy

Policy in this area has promoted the expanded use of agricultural chemicals and has, at the same time, been lax in dealing with health impacts. Many pesticides and synthetic fertilizers have been developed with public research monies, and their use has been touted by publicly funded extension workers and others in the vast agricultural bureaucracy. This push for chemical farming has not been balanced by a search for alternatives. For example, most official research and extension work has ignored the possibilities of low-input systems such as organic agriculture.

New directions

Because of threats to resource supplies, health and long-term productivity, the chemical path pursued in the second half of this century needs some redirection. Recommendations:

- Farmers should themselves pursue production alternatives which can reduce the need for chemical inputs.
- Public research and extension activities must aid farmers searching for alternatives. More attention at the federal, state and local levels should be given to organic farming demonstrations and research, and to practical training in organic practices.
- The full range of benefits in farm programs must be made available to the organic farmer, just as they are to the conventional operator. Some programs now require application of commercial fertilizers as a prerequisite to obtaining a loan.
- Safety standards for exposure to agricultural chemicals should be reviewed and strengthened. More research may also be needed on the long-term effects of exposure.

4 Glut of hunger: An analysis of federal food assistance programs

Policy decisions regarding food production ultimately play out in the marketplace. For most consumers, higher prices in the grocery store are an annoyance that may cause some alteration in buying habits. For low-income consumers, however, every increase in food costs pushes them one step closer to hunger.

In the early 1980s, the American public was shocked by news stories about the 're-emergence' of hunger in America. Soup lines and emergency food pantries reminiscent of the Great Depression spread from skid rows in big cities to small towns, suburbs and rural areas. Hunger – a problem many Americans thought had been eliminated by the War on Poverty of the 1960s – had returned to public consciousness.

Hunger is commonplace in the less-developed countries of the Third World, in countries which have been visited far too often by famine and chronic short supplies of food. But in the United States, a country whose farm economy has been burdened by price-depressing and chronic surpluses, the problem of hunger reflects a failure to allocate available resources to meet basic human needs.

The ranks of the poor have mushroomed over the past five years, reversing the downward trend of the preceding two decades. According to 1983 Census data, 15.2 percent of the population lives in poverty, up from 11.4 percent in 1978.

Poverty and hunger

Poverty and hunger have an interdependent relationship. In 1965, the poverty line was developed by combining a 1955 USDA nationwide food consumption survey showing that the average family spent one-third of its income on food, and a 1961 USDA study showing how little families could spend on food and still meet federally set nutrition standards. What resulted was a multiplication of this minimum food budget (originally called the Economy Food Plan, now the Thrifty Food Plan) by three. This became the 'poverty line' and has been adjusted every year since then, based on changes in the Consumer Price Index. Besides being out of date, the food budget used in the 1965 calculation reflects a diet that is just barely adequate – one described by the USDA itself as 'designed for short term use when funds are extremely low.'[1] Many people with food budgets at this level would obviously have trouble getting enough food, and those below the poverty line would surely have trouble.

Eligibility for participation in most federal assistance programs is based on the official poverty line. If eligibility is based on such an inadequate measure, a portion of the needy population is automatically ineligible for programs like food stamps or free and reduced price school meals. Yet, even using this inherently inadequate measure, the number of poor and hungry people is growing.

An even more sensitive indicator of just how poor those living below poverty have become is the 'poverty gap' (the total amount by which the incomes of all who are poor fall below the poverty threshold), which rose between 1981 and 1982 at an even faster pace than the poverty rate.[2] Americans are getting poorer at an alarming rate. The anti-poverty programs now in place do not reach all people in need and do not provide benefit levels high enough to allow those they do reach to escape poverty.

Despite these statistics, the Reagan Administration contends that the current method of counting the poor overstates the number because non-cash benefits such as food stamps, housing and medical assistance are not included as 'income.' But a February 1984 Census Bureau study indicated that while counting in-kind benefits would reduce the size of the poverty population and the poverty rate, the rate of increase in poverty between 1979 and 1982 would actually be higher with in-kind benefits included in the calculation.[3] When only cash is counted, the rate of increase in the numbers of poor was 28 percent, but when cash *and* in-kind benefits were counted the rate of increase ranged between 37 and 47 percent, depending on the monetary values assigned to non-cash benefits.[4] Why the disparity? Non-cash benefits were 10 percent lower in 1982 than in 1979. Budget cuts during this period disproportionately hurt the poorest of the poor and dramatically increased the 'poverty gap.' In short, more people became poorer.

Finally, when the poverty line was developed, people with poverty-level incomes were not subject to federal income tax. This is not the case today. According to Census Bureau data, the 1982 poverty rate would increase by 3.2 million people – from 15 percent to 16.4 percent – if computations were based on after-tax income.[5]

The social safety net

In no state in the continental U.S. does the combination of Aid to Families with Dependent Children (AFDC) – our basic welfare program – and food stamp benefits reach the federal poverty line.[6] In half the states, two-parent households are ineligible for AFDC regardless of employment status or income level. In no state is a single person who is not elderly or disabled eligible for federal cash welfare payments. There is, in fact, no 'safety net' which keeps all Americans from poverty.

The following factors exacerbate the situation:

- Cuts in vital programs such as AFDC and unemployment insurance have reduced the incomes of poor families. The Congressional Research Service estimates the drop in AFDC at 36 percent from 1970 to 1983.[7]
- Loss of coverage and cuts in medical assistance programs mean more disposable income is spent on health care and health emergencies.
- Unemployment increased from an average of 6.8 percent in 1980 to an average of 10.1 percent in 1983.[8] Yet only 38 percent of the currently unemployed receive unemployment insurance benefits, as a result of cuts in the period covered by benefits and longer duration unemployment brought on by recession.[9]
- Energy Department data show that oil price increases of the mid- and late 1970s have forced low-income households to spend several hundred percent more on home energy costs. Federal energy assistance programs have offset only one-third of this increase.[10]
- Food prices increased by 15 percent between 1980 and 1983.[11]
- USDA, in tabulating statistics and characteristics of food stamp households from 1975 to 1981, shows that the real income of the food stamp population as a whole has dropped dramatically.[12]

On top of all these economic factors, the poor suffered from cuts in federal food assistance programs. With the passage of the 1981 Omnibus Budget and Reconciliation Act (OBRA), deep cuts were made in food stamp and child nutrition programs. Contrary to Administration claims, these cuts did not eliminate 'fraud and abuse,' but were instead direct eligibility and benefit cuts.

According to a 1983 Congressional Budget Office (CBO) study, food stamps were to be cut by $7 billion (or 13 percent) between 1982 and 1985.[13] The Washington-based Center on Budget and Policy Priorities estimates two-thirds of these cuts came from recipients with incomes below the poverty level.[14] CBO also estimated cuts in child nutrition programs between fiscal years 1982 and 1985 at $5.2 billion (28 percent).[15] According to the Center on Budget and Policy Priorities, half of these cuts came from low-income children.[16] In addition, over 2,000 schools withdrew completely from the lunch program as a result of the problems created by curtailed subsidies.[17]

This constellation of factors translates into a hunger crisis. More people are poor; the programs which once helped them have been sharply cut, meaning fewer people eligible for assistance and reduced benefits for those still receiving aid.

Without federal programs, growing numbers of poor and hungry people have turned to the private sector for help. Across the U.S., lines at soup kitchens, food pantries and emergency food services doubled and tripled. But the private sector – churches, social service agencies and other organizations – realized that the need left by new and growing holes in the safety net could not be met by private charity alone.

Myriad reports and studies confirm this. In October 1982 the U.S. Conference of Mayors spoke out, saying that the need for food in American cities was a serious and growing problem.[18] A second mayors' report, issued in mid-1983, found the hunger problem unabated.[19] A 1983 report commissioned by the USDA found the number of hungry people 'increasing at a frantic pace and . . . the emergency food available for distribution . . . quickly depleted.'[20]

A U.S. General Accounting Office (GAO) study, *Public and Private Efforts to Feed America's Poor*, found that 'No longer are food centers serving only their traditional clientele of the chronically poor, derelicts, alcoholics and mentally ill persons . . . [but the] "new poor" are contributing to the increasing numbers seeking assistance.'[21] Numerous local, state and national anti-hunger organizations have conducted their own studies of hunger: all confirm that the problem is reaching crisis proportions.

A 1984 Harvard School of Public Health study looked at

hunger in New England and made a series of observations that doubtless hold true for the whole nation:

- Evidence of hunger exists in every state studied.
- Hunger is widespread and is increasing.
- Americans from many different socio-economic groups are hungry.
- There is evidence of human growth failure resulting from malnutrition.
- Hunger and the poverty from which it stems assault the human spirit and rip apart the structures of family and community.
- Hunger is the result of clear and conscious actions by government leaders.
- Ideology and rhetoric cloud the issues and ignore the seriousness of hunger.[22]

This ideology and rhetoric shapes the environment in which attempts to reform federal food assistance programs take place. Understanding some of the history of the development of social welfare systems is helpful when undertaking any type of welfare reform. These systems still are shaped by society's conception of who is 'worthy' of assistance: assistance should be unpleasant and difficult to obtain or it will discourage people from working.

Originally, assistance to the needy was a matter of private charity based on religious belief. The roots of a standardized welfare system began to develop in England, as a result of severe labor shortages following the Plague which struck the country in 1348. The 1349 Statute of Laborers forbade the giving of alms to so-called 'valient' beggars (the able-bodied) so as to compel them to work, restricted 'impotent' beggars and the unemployed to their place of origin (so as to retain local responsibility for the poor), and compelled the unemployed to work for any employer willing to hire them.

By the end of the fifteenth century, pregnant women, the very sick and the poor over age sixty were included among the 'impotent' poor. In 1601 these concepts were codified into the Elizabethan Poor Laws which mandated that while the 'impotent' adult poor could receive relief in their homes, the able-bodied poor were subject to the almshouse or workhouse.

The concepts exemplified by these laws dominated public assistance systems for the next three centuries, and still influence policy decisions and public opinion. While today there is a trend toward public assistance as a legal right, an acknowledgment of a government responsibility for certain basic necessities, and a broader definition of the 'worthy' poor, this trend is relatively new.

A broad federal role was not accepted in the United States until the Great Depression of the 1930s, when the enormous numbers of needy people defied a sharp distinction between the 'worthy' and 'un-worthy.' The next step forward did not come until the War on Poverty of the 1960s expanded welfare programs again.

With the reforms of the Reagan Administration, the nation has regressed to earlier conceptions of social welfare: a sharp demarcation between the truly needy (the worthy poor) and all others, and a diminution of federal responsibility in favor of less adequate local authority.

Despite historical antagonism to welfare reform, the issue of hunger received widespread media attention in 1983 and 1984. Public opinion has become increasingly sympathetic to the needs of hungry people. For example, a Lou Harris survey conducted in January 1984 found that 70 percent of those polled are 'now convinced that hunger in the country is a serious problem,' and 76 percent agreed that 'because the number of Americans in poverty has gone from 41 to 47 million people in two years, you can be sure that there are many . . . going hungry.'[23]

Problems which are poverty-related cannot be solved by changes in federal food assistance programs alone. Improving these programs can significantly reduce hunger and malnutrition, but can only begin to address the more far-reaching problem of poverty. Until longer-term solutions are found, however, federal food programs will continue to provide the first line of defense against hunger. For the present, we must look at the inadequacies and inequities in those programs and provide ideas for significant and meaningful reform. These reforms must be seen as incremental steps towards a complete solution to the problem of poverty.

THE FOOD STAMP PROGRAM

Present policy

The idea for a food stamp program was born in the late 1930s, with a limited program in effect from 1939 to 1943, and a pilot program revived in 1961. However, it wasn't until 1974 that the Food Stamp Program began to operate throughout the United States and territories based on a uniform set of federal rules. Before 1977 the program placed equal emphasis on using the country's agricultural surpluses and on raising levels of nutrition among low-income households. When the Food Stamp Act was revised in 1977, Congress also revised the purpose of the program to place greater emphasis on the anti-hunger aspect and to downgrade use of surpluses as a program goal.

Food stamp coupons are issued by the U.S. Department of Agriculture through state social services or welfare agencies. They may be used like cash to purchase food and seeds at stores which are authorized to accept them. They cannot be used to buy tobacco, cleaning items, alcohol and any non-edible product. Food stamps are provided to 'households,' defined as people who buy and prepare food together. The amount of stamps a household receives varies according to the household size and income. The smaller the income, the larger the food stamp benefit and vice versa.

In 1984 the program will cost about $11.6 billion, compared to $4.5 billion in 1975. In 1984, 21 million persons will receive benefits, up from 17 million in 1975. Since 1977 Congress has responded to program growth by pursuing 'reforms' which result in reduced benefits or entitlements to those benefits or in a more complex program.

To qualify for food stamps, one must have a low income and few financial assets. Households on welfare or Supplemental Security Income (SSI) are usually (but not always) eligible for food stamps, as are working families who, because of low wages or large size, need extra help to purchase enough food.

In 1981 over one million people lost their entitlement to food stamp benefits because Congress tightened income eligibility. Almost all were families with earned income just above the poverty level. Unemployed households are often ineligible for Food Stamp Program benefits because their assets exceed allowable levels since possessions like a car count as an asset. Moreover, while income eligibility levels are adjusted annually for inflation, asset limits are not.

Besides income and resource eligibility requirements, Food Stamp Program participants must also be U.S. citizens or aliens with permanent residence status, comply with the program's work requirements, and furnish social security numbers for all household members. Congress has made special concessions for persons who are elderly or disabled. Participation by college students and persons on strike is restricted; such persons must meet additional eligibility requirements.

Every county in a state must participate in the Food Stamp Program. Nationally, about 21 million persons use food stamps in the fifty states, District of Columbia, and the U.S. territories. Puerto Rico no longer participates in the program. Since 1982 Congress has given Puerto Rico a block grant to design and operate a nutrition assistance program for low-income Puerto Ricans.

Of current Food Stamp Program participants, over half

are children and 9 percent are elderly. Of the close to eight million households participating in the program, 76 percent of all households with children are headed by a woman. More than one-quarter of all food stamp households include a member who is either elderly or disabled.

Sixty-five percent of all food stamp households have gross incomes lower than $400 a month. Ninety-five percent of all households have gross incomes below the poverty line; 42 percent of all households have gross incomes below 50 percent of the poverty line. Ninety-six percent of participating households have less than $500 in assets – the 1982 average was $58. Seventy-five percent of all households have no assets.[24]

The average food stamp benefit is $1.41 per person per day, or 47 cents per meal. A family of four with no income receives $8.43 a day for food purchases, or $2.11 per person a day for food, or 70 cents per person per meal – the maximum food stamp allotment. Only 19 percent of food stamp households receive the maximum benefit.

Food stamp benefits are based on USDA's Thrifty Food Plan. The plan assumes that families obtain all of their food at average national prices, pay no sales tax (about one-third of the states apply their sales tax to food purchases), waste little and have the knowledge of nutritionists and home economists. It is the cheapest diet developed by the Department of Agriculture.

USDA looks at the cost of monthly food purchases for a family of four consisting of a man and woman aged twenty to fifty-four years of age, one child of six to eight years, and another of nine to eleven years. Food costs are then adjusted based on economy-of-scale factors meant to allow for per-person cost differences between large and small households. Food stamp coupon allotments are increased every October 1 based on the increase in the cost of food for the previous twelve-month period ending June 30. Therefore, by October 1, the food stamp coupon allotment is already three months out of date, and by September of the following year allotment levels are fifteen months out of date. For two years (fiscal years 1983 and 1984) food stamp recipients saw the value of the Thrifty Food Plan reduced by 1 percent, further restricting their ability to eat. Legislation passed at the close of the 98th Congress restored the full value of the Thrifty Food Plan. The maximum coupon allotment levels for November 1, 1984 to September 30, 1985, are:

Household size	1	2	3	4	5	6	7	8	each additional
Maximum coupon allotment	$79	145	208	264	313	376	416	475	+59

Note: Alaska, Hawaii, Guam and the Virgin Islands have higher allotment levels.

The program assumes the food stamp household will spend 30 percent of its income on food. This means that 30 percent of the household income, after certain deductions are taken, is subtracted from the Thrifty Food Plan. The difference is what the household receives in food stamp coupons. In today's economy it becomes increasingly difficult for a family to allot 30 percent of its income to food purchases. Even the President's Task Force on Food Assistance, in its January 1984 report, notes that 'many families have faced increasing pressures on available cash reserves in recent years due to dramatically rising energy prices, unemployment, and the inability of public assistance payments in many states to keep up with inflation.'[25]

There has been a substantial erosion in the benefit level of the Food Stamp Program itself, a large erosion of expendable cash income for all necessities, and a sharp economic recession. This erosion can only be curbed through substantial program reform to increase benefits to households living near or below poverty. In addition, there are serious questions about the the nutritional adequacy of the Thrifty Food Plan. Even the Department of Agriculture has recognized the nutritional problems posed by the plan. In early 1980, USDA noted:

> a number of factors make it difficult for many families to obtain an adequate diet on the amount of money which represents the cost of the Thrifty Food Plan. In fact, data on food consumption among low income households indicate that fewer than one in ten families spending an amount of money equivalent to the cost of the Thrifty Food Plan received 100 percent of the Recommended Daily Allowances. . . . The average food purchaser without specific nutritional skills and training would find it difficult to make the food choices which provide an adequate diet on the amount of money which represents the cost of the plan. (45 Fed. Reg. 22001 [1980])

According to the USDA's 1977-78 Nationwide Food Consumption Survey, only about 12 percent of the families spending at the level of the Thrifty Food Plan were able to obtain an adequate diet.[26]

In the summer of 1983, the Food Research and Action Center (FRAC) carried out a survey of 1,023 people coming into twenty-seven emergency food centers in fourteen states.[27] The study found that nearly two-thirds of those surveyed already used food stamps, but over three-fourths (77 percent) of those using food stamps had run out of food stamps by the third week of the month. Because their food stamps were inadequate, these recipients were dependent on soup kitchens or church pantries. Similar results were reported in late 1983 by the Maryland Food Committee,[28] and in the on-going (now in its sixth year) study of families with children and food emergencies being carried out by the East Harlem Interfaith Welfare Committee.

In sum, Food Stamp Program benefits are not a guarantee that even the most knowledgeable and conscientious recipient will obtain a nutritionally adequate diet. While the Food Stamp Program fulfills its statutory purpose of permitting recipients to obtain 'a more nutritious diet,' another statutory purpose – alleviating hunger and malnutrition – is not being fulfilled by the present program.

The Food Stamp Program is one of the few entitlement programs – that is, anyone is eligible as long as their income and resources fall below allowable limits. Consequently, a critical question in the Food Stamp Program is: When does the lack of income or resources limit the ability of households to obtain a nutritious diet? Prior to 1981, a household's net income (that is, income after certain deductions – principally for child care and excessive shelter costs – are taken) determined food stamp eligibility and benefits. But in 1981 Congress repealed the net income eligibility test in an effort 'to better target benefits to those who are most in need.'[29] Eligibility was limited to a gross income of 130 percent of the poverty line. (Elderly and disabled households, however, continued to have eligibility determined under the net income levels.) Then, in 1982, a second means test was added: recipients had to meet a net income test and a gross income test.

These Food Stamp Program cutbacks were particularly devastating for the working poor – households with part- or full-time workers who do not earn enough to feed their households without food stamps. Nearly one million people were eliminated from Food Stamp Program eligibility. Most were members of working households with gross incomes between 130 and 150 percent of the poverty line who had high shelter or child care costs. A simultaneous cutback in the deduction allowed from earned income resulted in reduced benefits for all remaining working households receiving food stamps, affecting 1½ million households containing about four million people.

An additional 1981 change further narrowed the scope of Food Stamp Program eligibility. Prior to 1981 any group of people living together who purchased and prepared their meals together for home consumption were treated as a separate household. Food stamp eligibility was based on the income and resources of all household members. In

1981 children of any age living with parents who were neither elderly nor disabled were prohibited from being treated as a separate household even if they purchased and prepared their meals separately from their parents. In 1982 this prohibition was extended to siblings living together.

These changes in the definition of a food stamp household drastically affected the ability of persons living below the poverty line to receive food stamps. It is very common for extended families to live together for financial reasons. Often the families sharing shelter are both living below poverty, but their combined incomes or resources put them above food stamp eligibility levels. This change in the law particularly hurt families who lost AFDC benefits under the 1981 budget cuts, and were forced to move into their parents' homes. While these AFDC families could continue to receive cash assistance under the AFDC program, many were not eligible for food stamps because their AFDC income combined with that of their parents put them above food stamp gross income eligibility levels.

Another factor determining Food Stamp Program eligibility is assets. Currently households are allowed to retain $1,500 in assets ($3,000 for elderly households). The value of the household's car in excess of $4,500 is counted toward the household's resource limit. The asset limitation amounts on all items but autos were established in 1971 and have never been updated. The asset limit applying to autos, established in 1975, has not been updated since 1977. Many households, especially the 'new poor' who have recently lost income due to unemployment, do not qualify for food stamps because they own too much. Sometimes these resources are not readily marketable in a depressed economy.

In sum, while large segments of the population are being dragged into poverty, many living at or near poverty are not eligible for food stamp benefits. Instead of expanding the universe of food stamp eligibles or at least seeing that eligibility criteria are adequately indexed to account for inflation, Congress has chosen to restrict eligibility further.

The tremendous increase in demand for emergency food from private sources is the logical consequence of this failure to meet the growing need for food assistance to low-income families, but even the most extraordinary efforts of the private sector have been unable to meet the demand.

In 1983, 47.1 million Americans fell below the poverty line or were 'near poor' (incomes not exceeding 125 percent of the poverty line). The poor and 'near poor' count is a good indication of the numbers of individuals 'at risk' of hunger, and, hence, potential participants in the Food Stamp Program. But participation has not kept pace with the increase in people in poverty.

Since food stamp eligibility is based at 130 percent of poverty, one can deduce from poverty data the number of persons eligible for, but not participating in, the Food Stamp Program. Roughly 60 percent of the eligible population participate in the Food Stamp Program. Participation is lowest among the elderly, where only 40-50 percent of the eligible elderly participate, and single person households (30-40 percent of eligibles). Participation is higher among families with very low income and families with children.[30]

Poor information concerning program eligibility status is the single most important barrier to participation.[31] In 1981 Congress not only repealed funding, but prohibited future funding for any Food Stamp Program outreach activities. Prior to 1981 states were obligated to conduct full-scale information programs about the availability, eligibility requirements, rules and benefits of the Food Stamp Program designed to reach every potentially eligible household. Besides these informational activities, outreach also included various forms of assistance to households in the application process, such as pre-screening of the application and transportation to the local food stamp office. The 1981 Budget Act ended funding for these activities.

There are other reasons for non-participation. For example, prior to 1979, many low-income persons did not participate in the Food Stamp Program because they were required to purchase their food stamps and did not have the available cash. Congress eliminated the purchase requirement in order to remove this bar to participation. Another reason is that the benefit to which a household is entitled may be so low that it is not worth the time and effort involved to obtain it, thus deterring participation.

Another obstacle to participation is the number of administrative hassles a household must endure in order to receive food stamps. Long waits, repeated trips to the food stamp office to document need, crowded waiting rooms, rude or condescending behavior by eligibility workers, and complicated forms, are all common occurrences. Or households which do establish their eligibility and receive benefits may later lose them as a result of an erroneous decision. These households, although still eligible for benefits, may never seek them again.

Getting to the food stamp office itself may be the most difficult aspect of program participation for some households. Many households lack transportation to a distant food stamp office. Other potential participants may not make it to the office because of age, physical condition or working hours. While there are currently provisions in the Food Stamp Act and regulations designed to improve access to the Food Stamp Program, these provisions are often not enforced.

The policy implications of these facts are straightforward. If we are truly interested in ending hunger in America, we must inform people about eligibility and eliminate barriers to participation. Families who lost their eligibility status in 1981 must be brought back into the program. They are just as needy now as they were before the 1981 Budget Act.

New directions

The need for reform in the Food Stamp Program centers on

two crucial components: adequacy of program benefits and expansion of eligibility. A third factor – image of the program – also merits discussion.

Adequacy of benefits

The Food Stamp Program is not designed to provide a nutritionally adequate diet for low-income Americans. Benefits are based on the inadequate Thrifty Food Plan and the assumption that participants have cash available to supplement their food stamps, which is usually not the case.

Perhaps the simplest way to make benefits adequate would be to revise the food plan on which benefits are based. USDA has computed the cost of a variety of food plans. The plan above the Thrifty Food Plan is called the Low-Cost Food Plan, and costs 27 percent more than the Thrifty Food Plan. There are several justifications for raising benefit levels by this amount. For example, despite the fact that households receiving food stamps have food shopping expertise 'as good as or better than that of other households'[32], only 12 percent of low-income households spending at the full food stamp allotment level are obtaining 100 percent of their Recommended Dietary Allowances (RDA)[33] and only 34 percent are obtaining 80 percent of these standards.[34]

The greatest percentage of low-income households spend between 110 and 149 percent of the cost of the Thrifty Food Plan on food – this is the level necessary for a *majority* of people to achieve even 80 percent of their RDAs.[35] For a majority to reach 100 percent of the RDAs, spending rises to between 150 and 199 percent of the Thrifty Food Plan.

The Food Research and Action Center's study, 'Still Hungry,' confirmed that food stamp recipients cannot supplement their stamps with cash, but are compelled to seek emergency assistance instead.[36] FRAC concluded that a 25 percent increase in benefits would improve participants' ability to obtain an adequate diet. This change would only raise the average per-meal benefit from 47 cents to 59 cents. If the standard upon which benefits are assessed were raised to an adequate level, the program could continue to provide greater benefits to households with lower incomes. The Low-Cost Food Plan could then be updated for inflation to maintain its adequacy relative to food prices. Even greater adequacy would, of course, be achieved with more frequent inflation adjustments – for example, every six months rather than annually.

Expansion of eligibility

Due to the many holes in the present social safety net, the Food Stamp Program takes on added significance as the only universal federal benefit program for the poor. In our current maze of federal, state and local programs serving different categories of people and varying widely across the country, food stamps often serve as an equalizer for poor people. In states with very low AFDC benefits, larger food stamp allotments help families by establishing something of a federal 'floor.' In many states, food stamps may be the only assistance available to two-parent families or single non-elderly or disabled adults. For these reasons, it is crucial that eligibility be made more inclusive. The recent changes in eligibility which supposedly targeted the program to the 'truly needy' in fact eliminated many who are still in dire need. Some suggestions:

● A return to basing eligibility on income *after* allowable deductions are taken, to more accurately target the program.
● Update asset limits. Even the President's Task Force on Food Assistance recommended increasing assets limits to $2,250 for non-elderly, non-disabled households ($3,500 for elderly and disabled households),

and vehicle value to $5,500. These modest limit increases would be an important step toward adequacy. In fact, just to keep pace with inflation, the original asset limit for non-elderly households would already be over $3,500 and car value would be over $7,700.

- Liberalize the number and amount of deductions used in determining eligibility and benefit levels to more accurately reflect the true circumstances of low-income people.
- Return the household definition to an economic unit and stop penalizing family members forced to share living space due to lack of income.

Image

The nation would greatly benefit from a public education campaign to improve the image of the Food Stamp and other public assistance programs. Public leaders should explain that people who use food stamps –

- Face hard times and lack of income, usually for a limited period of time.
- Are able to feed themselves and their families more adequately, thereby better maintaining health and preventing more costly medical care.
- Are, for the most part, economical shoppers.

Such messages could begin to dispel the myth of the 'welfare cheater' among policy-makers, the general public and the poor themselves.

WIC (SPECIAL SUPPLEMENTAL FOOD PROGRAM FOR WOMEN, INFANTS AND CHILDREN)

Present policy

The discovery of hunger in the United States during the late 1960s alerted the nation to the pernicious effects of poverty on the health and well-being of millions of low-income Americans. The most vulnerable individuals among the poor were found to be pregnant women, their infants and young children. In 1969, the White House Conference on Food, Nutrition and Health recommended that additional special attention be given to the nutritional needs of low-income pregnant women and preschool children. As a result, Congress in 1972 enacted the Special Supplemental Food Program for Women, Infants and Children, commonly referred to as WIC. Initially a $20 million pilot project, WIC provided nutritious food supplements, rudimentary health screening and nutrition education to pregnant, breastfeeding, and post-partum women and their children until age four. In 1974, WIC became a full-fledged national nutrition and health program. Coverage of children was extended to age five.

Although the WIC program does not enjoy permanent authorization by Congress, each of the four legislative extensions passed since 1974 has resulted in significant increases in participation. The authorization level has increased from $20 million in 1973 to $1.36 billion in fiscal year 1984. Participation has grown from 205,000 people in FY 1974 to just over three million in FY 1984.

Program operations

The WIC program is administered by the Food and Nutrition Service (FNS) of USDA. FNS provides cash grants to state health departments and federally recognized

Indian tribes to fully cover both food and administrative costs of program operations. The state health department coordinates WIC activities via the WIC state agency. The WIC state agency is responsible for implementation of all federal regulations, development of yearly plans of operation and distribution of funds to the local WIC agencies.

It is at the local agency level that direct participant contact is made and WIC food benefits are provided. The local WIC agency, which operates WIC clinics in a public health facility or other non-profit service agency, certifies women, infants, and children as program-eligible, based on both medical and economic needs. The medical indices used for certification include blood-iron levels, growth measures and dietary patterns. Once medical or nutritional need is established, the individual must also be certified to be at economic risk – at or below 185 percent of the poverty line.

The WIC program is both a remedial and a preventive effort aimed at the at-risk population. Services provided include:

- *Food packages* or vouchers for food packages designed to provide specific nutrients known to be lacking in the diets of the target population. WIC participants receive their supplemental foods in one of three ways: use of vouchers in food markets, direct delivery (usually via dairies) or direct distribution from clinics or warehouses.
- *Nutrition education*. At least one-sixth of the funds expended by the state agency for administrative costs must be spent for nutrition education.
- *Health Care*. Each WIC agency must insure that its clients have available and accessible health care.

Numerous research studies and USDA evaluations have made WIC the most studied and conspicuous public health program of its size. Much of the historic bi-partisan Congressional support for WIC is based on the positive findings of comparative studies of women and children receiving or not receiving WIC supplemental foods.

A 1984 GAO evaluation of all of the WIC research studies to date was done at the request of Senator Jesse Helms (R-NC), a frequent critic of the program. GAO found strong evidence to prove that WIC improves the outcome of pregnancy by reducing the incidence of low birth weight.[37] Positive evaluations of the program have been the program's major defense against Reagan Administration budget reduction proposals.

Despite a proven track record and strong political backing, WIC continues to be one of the only federal food assistance programs without entitlement status. Each fiscal year, WIC is given a specific, limited amount of funding and therefore cannot provide benefits to all of the eligible women, infants and children in the nation. In 1984, the approximately three million individuals who received WIC supplemental foods each month represented less than one-third of the estimated eligible population. According to the report of the President's Task Force on Food Assistance, about 25 percent of eligible women, 35-40 percent of eligible infants, and 20 percent of eligible children participate in the WIC program.[38]

This creates, at the local agency level, a kind of 'nutritional triage.' Due to the limited number of available places on the local WIC caseload, the WIC staff enrolls participants on a priority basis, with open program slots going to the highest-risk individuals (pregnant women and infants) first. Although this priority system of caseload management is designed to meet the medical and nutritional needs of those at greatest risk, it continues to leave large numbers of eligible high-risk persons unserved.

New directions

Recognizing the funding struggle of all social programs during the 1980s, two critical but modest steps could be taken to improve and expand WIC services without major legislative changes.

Integrate Maternal and Child Health Programs

Although the WIC program is operated by each state's department of health, the WIC staff is often isolated from other integrated maternal and child health services at both the state and local level. Even after a decade WIC often continues to operate tangentially to maternal and infant care projects and other public health services. In some instances, the result of this relationship has been poor state management of WIC, underutilization of available WIC funds, and underserving the eligible population. Better integration of WIC staff and program services into the maternal and child health structure at the state and local level should be a requirement for all WIC programs.

Appropriate full funding levels

Making WIC a full entitlement program, like the National School Lunch Program, would allow all eligible individuals to be served. Current problems such as waiting lists and caseload reductions to avoid overspending would be eliminated or improved. WIC might begin to reach its goals of improving pregnancy outcome, preventing nutritional problems in children and significantly reducing future health care costs.

To extend WIC benefits and services to the potentially eligible population would require a significant budget increase – nearly three times the current appropriation. This could not be done overnight, of course. But, to give financial stability to the current program and provide the groundwork for full entitlement in the future, legislation making WIC a capped entitlement program should be enacted to require full funding of authorized budgets. This fully appropriated status for WIC would be the initial step toward providing nutritional support, health screening and nutrition education to all women, infants and children in need.

CHILD NUTRITION

Present policy

In addition to WIC there are four major nutrition assistance programs for children: National School Breakfast and Lunch Programs, the Child Care Food Program and the Summer Food Service Program for Children.

The National School Breakfast and Lunch Programs

These provide financial assistance to schools so that all students can receive a nutritious lunch and/or breakfast. They enable low-income students to get meals at no cost or at a reduced price, and allow the schools to charge other students somewhat less than the full cost of the meal. In addition, food commodities are available to schools that participate in the programs. Nationally, USDA runs the programs; on the state level, the programs are run by the state department of education; and, on the local level, by school boards and school administration. They can usually be implemented without substantial cost to the school district.

Only 3.5 million (25 percent) needy children of the 11.5 million children receiving a free or reduced-price lunch have an opportunity to participate in the school breakfast program. Budget costs in FY 1982 forced 650 schools to drop out of the breakfast program and over 2,000 to drop out of the lunch program. While over 91,000 schools serving over 23 million students participate in the lunch program, only 34,000 schools serving 3.5 million students participate in the breakfast program.

USDA-sponsored studies have found that –

- Lunch program participants from low-income households depend on the lunch program for 34-49 percent of daily nutrient intake.[39]
- The school lunch program, as judged by the nutrient intake of students, clearly provides meals superior to the lunches received by non-participants.[40]
- The school breakfast program, because it delivers mostly free meals and is found predominantly in schools located in low-income areas, primarily serves the poor. Moreover, the school breakfast program increases the chance that children will eat a breakfast.[41] (The nutritional content of the school breakfast program is less than adequate, however: it provides only milk, bread or cereal, and fruit or fruit juice; no protein, such as eggs or cheese, is included.)
- The school lunch and breakfast programs provide food and are not income supplement programs. The federal subsidy increases the amount of food available to a family, but does not increase discretionary income.
- The school breakfast program helps children from low-income households more than it helps anyone else. Among low-income children ages six to eleven, participants consume 25 percent more of the RDA for calcium, 30 percent more of the riboflavin RDA, 15 percent more of the vitamin B6 RDA, and 85 percent more of the vitamin C RDA than do children who eat other types of breakfast.[42]

New directions
Legislative options at the federal and state levels for the school breakfast program include:

- Improving the quality of the meal pattern by increasing the rate of reimbursement for meals that serve additional protein and a wider variety of fruits, vegetables and grains.
- Providing financial incentives to schools to initiate a school breakfast program, such as assistance in purchasing food service equipment, higher rates of reimbursements for schools which state agencies have defined as 'in special need of assistance,' and providing federal commodities to school breakfast programs.
- Requiring any school where 25 percent or more of the children receive free or reduced-price lunches to institute a school breakfast program.

Legislative options for the school lunch program include:

- Making chiildren from families at 135 percent of poverty level eligible for free meals and those from families at 195 percent of poverty level eligible for reduced-price lunches.
- Restoring the $1 billion cut in program expenditures initiated by the Reagan Administration in FY 1982.

A longer-range goal is a universal free lunch. Today, approximately 50 percent of the lunches served through the National School Lunch Program are to children who qualify for free or reduced-price lunch, creating a three-part system of paid, reduced-price and free lunches. This three-part system requires school administrators to document and verify the incomes of applicants for free or reduced-price meals. In the process, poor children are often made to feel 'different' – stigmatized and unworthy. Frequently, these children or their parents decide not to participate rather than be publicly identified.

All children should have an opportunity to participate in school lunch and breakfast programs. A school lunch program for all children could have several significant advantages. First, it would end the necessity of having to document and verify the income of children within the school. Second, it would refocus the program on its initial goal of providing nutritious meals to all children throughout the nation. Third, it would eliminate all problems associated with overt identification of poor children.

The Child Care Food Program (CCFP)

This provides federal funds to organized child care programs so that all children up to twelve years old (and handicapped children of any age) can receive nutritious breakfasts, lunches, suppers or snacks. Funding is unlimited, and all eligible children have a right to participate. Federal meal reimbursements cover all, or most, of the meal and administrative costs. In addition, sponsors may receive USDA food commodities (or a cash equivalent). Currently 250,000 children are served by family day care providers, while over 750,000 children attend child care centers. Funding for the program was cut by 30 percent ($130 million) in FY 1982.

The need for accessible, quality and affordable child care is increasing daily. Over 40 percent of mothers of one-year-old children work, and 57 percent of mothers of children between three and five. CCFP helps to keep child care affordable for these parents. A survey of CCFP sponsors in the Northeast found that 'the availability of CCFP funds has enabled many providers to remain in operation and to keep their fees at an affordable level. The accessibility of affordable day care has freed many families from low income status.'[43]

CCFP has helped to provide low-income children with better meals. A USDA-funded report on the program found major differences between participating and non-participating day care centers:

> For every measure examined, participating centers have statistically significantly higher levels of meal quality than non-

participating centers. Equally striking is the finding that participating family day care homes also serve meals of superior nutritional quality, and these meals generally contain foods of higher qality and variety than those served by non-participating centers.[44]

New directions
Legislative options:

- Establishing an outreach campaign requirement for state agencies to find accessible, quality and affordable care for low-income working parents and to bring more family day care homes and centers into CCFP.
- Restoring the $130 million in program cuts initiated by the Reagan Administration in FY 1982.
- Establishing a tax credit system for private industries that set up non-profit, licensed day care facilities which participate in CCFP.

The Summer Food Service Program for Children (SFSPC)

This is designed to feed children up to eighteen years old during the summer months when school food services are not available. The program must be free and is entirely funded by the federal government and administered by USDA through state departments of education or USDA regional offices. Any school food authority, public agency or residential camp may be a sponsor and is reimbursed for the meals served to eligible children.

In 1983, approximately 1.2 million children participated in the program. Participation dropped by 500,000 children when the Administration was successful in 1981 in preventing private non-profit agencies from sponsoring a program.

The SFSPC has the same nutrition standards as the National School Lunch Program. It makes good sense to provide a program which gives low-income children year-round good nutrition.

New directions
- Allow private non-profit sponsors serving areas where one-third or more of the population is low-income to participate in the program.
- Create a nutrition education component in SFSPC by providing stipends for community nutrition students who provide materials and services to program sponsors, and education to children.

NUTRITION PROGRAMS FOR THE ELDERLY

Present policy

Two federal nutrition programs address the special needs of the elderly: congregate meals and home-delivered meals. These programs were incorporated into the Older Americans Act in 1972 both to improve the diet of older persons and to help eliminate isolation.

In authorizing these programs Congress recognized that

> Many elderly persons do not eat adequately because (1) they cannot afford to do so; (2) they lack the skills to select and prepare nourishing and well-balanced meals; (3) they have limited mobility which may impair their capacity to shop and cook for themselves; and (4) they have feelings of rejection and loneliness which obliterate the incentive necessary to prepare and eat a meal alone. These and other physiological, psychological, social, and economic changes that occur with aging result in a pattern of living which causes malnutrition and further physical and mental deterioration.[45]

The senior nutrition programs are not entitlements; due to limited funding, they fail to serve all eligible seniors. Although the law forbids means tests, it does establish priority service guidelines. Preference is given to persons with the 'greatest economic or social needs.'[46] Economic need is defined as income below the poverty line; social need includes factors such as physical and mental disabilities, language barriers, isolation and minority status which may threaten independence.[47]

While congregate meals, served in group settings, usually at lunch, are open to any person aged sixty or older (and that person's spouse of any age), home-delivered meals are restricted to home-bound elders who are too ill or frail to attend a congregate site. Altogether, over three million elders participate in congregate meals and over 600,000 in home-delivered meals, for a total consumption of over 200 million meals in fiscal year 1983.[48]

The structure of the programs may be something of a mixed blessing. The fact that they are not strictly programs for the poor accords them greater political support than most 'welfare' programs and frees them of the stigma many elders associate with means-tested programs. Conversely, they are less effective than other programs in reaching their target population – persons with greatest social and economic need. While between one-half and two-thirds of program participants are low-income, these approximately two million persons constitute only 43 percent of the 4.9 million people over fifty-nine with incomes below the poverty line.[49] Minority participation in the program is less than 20 percent. This is substantially lower than the incidence of poverty among minority elders: 38.2 percent among blacks and 26.6 percent among Hispanics.[50]

Despite these shortcomings, the programs have helped improve the nutritional intake of participants, particularly among the poor. A report for the Department of Health and Human Services notes: 'Consumption of a program meal elevated dietary intakes among poorer elderly respondents so that it was comparable to intakes of more affluent respondents.'[51]

New directions

These programs could be improved significantly without major restructuring. First, the level at which funding for the programs is appropriated is seriously inadequate. Second, the statutory language which makes service to the neediest elders a priority is not vigorously enforced.

The simplest means of expanding service would be to accord entitlement status to these programs and appropriate sufficient funds to serve all elders requesting service. Short of entitlement status, additional program funds specifically targeted for program expansion to unserved low-income seniors could greatly improve the program without destroying its broad base of support.

Appropriations for these programs have failed to keep pace with inflation, and they have fallen behind the rapidly growing aging population. According to a 1983 Census report: 'The 65 and over population grew twice as fast as the rest of the population in the last two decades.'[52] Census projections indicate that the aging population will continue to grow more rapidly than the total population for the next fifty years.

Programs such as the senior meals programs can play a vital role in helping the aging population live independently and maintain their health for longer periods of time. Without such support, the resultant health costs and institutional care would be greater than the investment in the present represented by programs like these nutrition programs for the elderly.

THE NEED FOR A NATIONAL NUTRITION CENTER

A major information gap faces federal administrators, Congressional representatives and local policy-makers concerned about the nutritional status of the U.S. population. They have no way of gauging, or even estimating, the impact of policy decisions on hunger. At the present time, there is no agency in government that examines:

- Prospective and actual impacts of economic trends on the nutritional health of the population.
- Potential and actual impacts of federal budget and policy decisions affecting food, nutrition and health programs on the nutritional health of the population.
- Potential and actual impacts of food processing, food marketing, and food retailing and agriculture-related decisions on the nutritional health of the population.

Much of the information needed to carry out these analyses is available, but spread out among a number of government agencies and divisions within the agencies. However, there is a great need to collect, integrate and analyze it in a practical and policy-oriented way that is useful to decision-makers. These analyses would be very useful to policy-makers. They would be, in essence, nutritional impact statements.

These nutritional impact statements could look at the broad issue of nutritional health, incorporating:

- Undernutrition among specific population groups – particularly as it relates to being poor, but also as it relates to being at risk for other reasons, e.g., the barriers to adequate nutrition related to increasing age.
- Overnutrition – levels of nutrients (e.g., salt or saturated fat) which are so high in the diet that they lead to increased morbidity and mortality.
- Underconsumption of particular nutrients (e.g., zinc, fiber, etc.) because of the make-up of the food supply or broadly practiced food habits unrelated to poverty.
- Lack of an accessible and affordable food supply because of economic and environmental conditions

which affect all individuals, e.g., policies affecting soil, water use, energy costs, pesticides, etc.

There has never been a focal point in government, an institution that brings all food-related policy decisions back to the most important bottom line – the nutritional health of human beings. After all, the ultimate purpose of food production should be the 'cultivation' of healthy people.

A quasi-independent government National Nutrition Center could serve as just such a focal point. This center could collect and integrate existing information from widespread sources into meaningful analyses. It would focus on nutritional impact alone and would be staffed by experts in the fields of nutrition and health; agriculture; food processing, marketing, and retailing; and economics and statistics. It would be a non-partisan agency, developing and analyzing issues objectively.

The National Nutrition Center would develop policy questions, analyze available data, and produce and regularly distribute formal reports. It could also prepare reports on critical nutrition issues for key Congressional committees. The reports would be made available to the public.

The Center would –

● Analyze the impact on the nutritional health of the U.S. population of predicted, proposed or actual economic trends; agriculture and food processing/marketing/retailing policies; and federal budget and policy decisions in the area of food, nutrition, and health programs.
● Report these analyses to Congress and the public.
● Determine 'information gaps' in research relevant to policy decisions on nutrition and report to Congress.
● Develop nutrition indices to be reported to Congress and the public, which would indicate progress in improving the nutritional health of the nation.

Given current research and monitoring systems, a very important set of data – timely and useful information on the food consumption and nutritional status of our population (including where and why people are mal-nourished) – does not exist. The three major nutrition monitoring systems – the Department of Health and Human Services' Health and Nutrition Examination Survey (HANES), USDA's Nationwide Food Consumption Survey, and the Center for Disease Control's voluntary collection of data from public health clinics – are not coordinated or comparable, do not provide data on *current* nutritional status or food consumption, and reveal little on a local, state or regional level, or about high risk groups. Under the Reagan Administration their budgets have been threatened and their continuation delayed and/or cut back.

COMMODITY DISTRIBUTION

Present policy

Historically, commodity distribution has included manda-tory distribution of USDA commodity foods in programs such as school lunch and breakfast programs, the elderly nutrition programs, and supplemental food programs (especially the Commodity Supplemental Food Program, which operates as a substitute for WIC in certain areas). Commodity donations are also made to the Needy Family Program for Indians and residents of the Pacific Trust Territories, charitable institutions and summer camps. In addition to the regular commodities, the Secretary of Agriculture may donate 'bonus' commodities at his discre-tion. Traditionally, the Department has donated food only to organizations already participating in its food programs.

There are two sources of commodities. Section 32

commodities are purchased and distributed using funds obtained from U.S. Customs duties. These commodities are generally purchased during temporary surplus periods at harvest and distributed to food assistance program participants. Comprising such items as meat, poultry, fruits and vegetables, these commodities are not stored. Section 416 commodities are obtained from the stocks of commodities purchased under the price support programs, and generally include cheese, butter, non-fat dry milk, wheat, corn and honey.

The major legislative change in the Commodities Distribution Program came in 1981 with the creation of the Special Food Distribution Program. Under this program, the government provides food that can be distributed to persons for use in their homes, through distribution channels established by the states. This distribution was authorized by the Agriculture and Food Act of 1981, which lifted the prohibition against donating food for use in the home. (A precursor pilot program in 1980 permitted the donation of food to selected food banks.) The moving force behind this distribution was huge surplus dairy products in government stockpiles. Only when these products were in danger of spoiling, and the U.S. could not find a buyer for them, did Congress and the President act to distribute surplus food to a growing number of needy Americans.

The first distribution of cheese and butter began in January 1982. The distribution of dairy products has continued, and other staple commodities (non-fat dry milk, honey, corn meal and flour) have been added. In 1983, $932 million worth of commodities were distributed. The Temporary Emergency Food Assistance Act of 1983 required the Agriculture Department to distribute any Commodity Credit Corporation commodities in excess of those required for other activities (PIK, world trade, international food aid). The Act also set aside $50 million to pay distribution costs. In September 1983, the special distribution program was extended through FY 1985.

Returning to the commodity program for family food assistance is a giant step backward – to a program in which the poor are the overflow safety valve, consuming foods produced in excess. Unlike the Food Stamp Program, which recognizes that people have the right to an adequate diet and the right to choose what to eat, commodity distribution compels poor people to eat America's leftovers.

Nutrition and food consumption surveys tell us whether the commodity and food stamp programs improve the nutritional well-being of poor people. The 1965 USDA nationwide household food consumption survey, conducted before the Food Stamp Program became national in scope, found that less than 10 percent of households spending at the lowest level for food purchases had adequate diets.[53] In 1967, Field Foundation medical teams investigating the extent of hunger in the United States found cases of severe malnutrition as well as widespread illness and undernutrition among poor people.[54] During the period in which these surveys were conducted, commodities were the primary vehicle for federal food assistance to families.

Ten years later, the situation was different. USDA's food consumption survey found that low-income people had much better diets than in 1965.[55] A 1977 Field Foundation follow-up found much less evidence of severe malnutrition in the poverty areas visited ten years earlier.[56] Poverty still existed; the food programs were meeting only bare subsistence needs; but people at least had some food and were in better physical condition. Food stamps made the primary difference.

Foods stockpiled because of overproduction and farm commodities which are purchased by the government as a way to boost prices may indeed be components of a nutritionally adequate diet. However, if nutritional adequacy is the goal, then nutritional needs (including individual variations), nutrient content of foods and accessibility should be the primary considerations of any commodity distribution program.

New directions

The farm economy periodically generates surpluses even with price-support programs. These surpluses often occur in times of high unemployment and, hence, when the need for food assistance is greatest.

Distribution of government-purchased surplus commodities through local charitable organizations is cumbersome, often poorly targeted, available only in limited locations and at times wasteful. (Commodities often deteriorate by the time they reach the poor who, in turn, do not have the facilities to store them properly.) Further, industry representatives have charged that commodity distribution displaces commercial sales.

These problems, combined with the problem of the inadequacy of food stamp benefits, could be addressed by a surplus commodity supplemental food stamp program. Such a program would provide free supplemental food coupons to food stamp recipients and would supplement, not replace, benefits provided under the Food Stamp Program. This would assure targeting to the neediest persons and provide income verification at no additional cost to the state or federal government.

The coupons would have a quantity value (e.g., one gallon of milk). Coupons would expire after a set period of time in order to prevent stockpiling. They would be used solely to purchase USDA-designated surplus commodities – principally the Section 416 commodities, e.g., milk, cheese, butter, rice, corn meal and honey. (This is similar to the current WIC vouchers, which are redeemed in grocery stores for specific nutritious foods.) These coupons would be used in normal channels of trade – retail grocery stores. Thus, the program would use and support existing food distribution systems instead of creating new ones. In addition, needy recipients would have better access to commodities at convenient times and places. This is especially important to rural people and the working poor.

The program would increase demand for specific surplus

agriculture products. Availability of the vouchers would be 'triggered' when government purchases reached a statutorily designated level. The need for storage facilities and administrative structures required under federal commodities purchase programs, and hence the cost of these programs, would be diminished. In the case of milk, the cost of processing from fluid to dry milk would also be eliminated. Additional cost savings would be realized by eliminating state and federal storage costs and the further processing and distribution once states receive surplus commodities.

5 World hunger, world markets

Among the great unmitigated tragedies of this inter-dependent world are mass human hunger and the near breakdown of equitable systems of international trade which could help to bring it under control.

These intertwined harbingers of global political-economic decay and its attendant revolutionary violence have become progressively more apparent since shortly after World War II. Beginning in the early 1950s, the response of the U.S. and other affluent Western nations to this worsening crisis has been a jerry-built structure of foreign aid and trade programs widely publicized as devices for helping the less-developed countries (LDCs) to improve their peoples' condition. At the same time it has been no secret, so far as U.S. participation is concerned at least, that another purpose of these policies is the expansion of U.S. markets and U.S. political and military influence around the world.

Not surprisingly, these goals and purposes have often proved contradictory, and the programs themselves have created more problems than they have resolved for donor and recipient nations alike. World hunger will not go away. After two generations of 'aid and trade' programs and promotions, almost one billion people – a fourth of the world's population – are either starving to death or 'chronically undernourished.'[1]

Clearly, given the fact that human beings must eat to live, the tragedy of world hunger and the poverty which causes it is intimately related to distortions in national and international systems governing the production and distribution of food. For poor subsistence farmers, agriculture inevitably is a life or death occupation, but when mishandled it also can damage its most affluent practitioner.

When American agricultural surpluses began to accumulate in unmanageable amounts in the early 1950s, it was determined by successive Administrations that a massive program of government support for the sale or donation of agricultural products to the hungry nations, as well as to anyone else who would buy, was essential for the health of this country's farm economy. Private interest groups and politicians also saw that the programs would receive broad popular support as an admirable humanitarian cause, making them easy to push through Congress during a period when Americans were feeling especially prosperous and generous. The programs also paid off handsomely for American interests in a position to take advantage of them. By the late 1970s about 70 percent of aid money provided to the LDCs was being spent on U.S. goods and services. Since 1950, over $30 billion of this assistance has been for long-term, low-interest concessional (subsidized) sales or grant food shipments.

The flood of U.S. food exported under foreign aid auspices, particularly grain, appears from evidence available now to have been of discouragingly little help to the average American farmer, but of considerable benefit to four other groups: large American agribusiness producers, the major grain trading companies, foreign governments and foreign business complexes. The Third World's poor and hungry, on the other hand, have benefited relatively little either from food aid or from other types of U.S. support. On the contrary, the income gap between developed and underdeveloped countries has widened over the past twenty years, and the Third World is now experiencing its worst economic crisis since the great Depression of the 1930s, staggering under an accumulated debt approaching $1 trillion. Most disturbing of all, the living standards of the poor in most of the LDCs have failed to improve appreciably, contributing to mounting social tensions.

A frequently proposed remedy for this situation is to change the traditional 'trade and aid' slogan of the American foreign development bureaucracy to 'trade *not* aid,' thereby emphasizing the virtues of self-reliance over handouts. Unfortunately, 'trade not aid' necessarily implies a willingness on the part of the U.S. to buy more of the Third World's goods at more generous prices, a condition we have so far been unwilling or unable to fulfill. Nor has there been much enthusiasm in this country or in most of the LDCs for the healthy notion that poor countries should encourage the cultivation of more food for local consumption rather than for export. LDC governments and landowners find that it better serves their interests to accept food aid rather than to undertake the redistribution of their own farm lands, energy supplies and other inputs necessary to achieve agricultural self-reliance.

This is not to say that American agricultural exports are wicked or otherwise undesirable. Indeed, as the world is at present structured they are essential, and their curtailment would produce chaos. The U.S. by 1980 accounted for 64 percent of world grain shipments, a critical contribution to humanity's breadbasket.[2] The damage caused by this export bonanza has not resulted from the sharing of U.S. agricultural productivity with the rest of the world, but from the private systems and public policies under which the exchange is conducted.

The following pages discuss first the financing, control and regulation of agricultural export programs within the U.S., and then the impact of these practices on the poorer nations of the world.

How government subsidies yield profits for traders

Most American food produced for export and its sale

abroad is subsidized, directly or indirectly, in a myriad of different ways, by the U.S. government. This means that producers, traders and shippers are to varying degrees publicly supported. However, these benefits are not equally bestowed along the chain from American fields to foreign consumers.

Agricultural analyst Richard Gilmore, a persistent critic of this state of affairs, and in particular of the clash of policies and interests which distort and destabilize the world grain trade, writes:

> Government remains the first and last link in the agricultural chain. Grain does not move from field to market through the magic of Adam Smith's 'invisible hand.' Instead, government is a principal in all phases of the grain trade from its origination on the farm to final delivery. No group in the agricultural chain, including the largest grain merchants, could prosper without some government assistance.[3]

When the issue of government supports is discussed in macro-economic terms, the results can be misleadingly cheering, the illusion being that because food exports improve the U.S. trade balance they must be good also for American family farmers. For example, between 1971 and 1981, U.S. farm exports – the most important being corn, wheat and soybeans – expanded six times in value, to $44 billion, and tripled in volume. By 1980 more than one-third of harvested U.S. acreage was being exported, and in 1981 there was a $26.5 billion surplus in food exports over food imports.[4]

This export boom has helped to cushion U.S. foreign trade deficits chalked up in other categories of commerce, but has been hazardous for farmers, who now find themselves dependent on the financial props provided by government in support of foreign sales and grants to the Third World, which peaked in the mid-1970s. Sales to the world as a whole continued to rise until 1981. Over the years these sales have taken on the aura of guaranteed markets, encouraging increases in production which are difficult to reverse. Downturns recorded in foreign sales in 1982-83, despite continuing government support, have seriously aggravated the farm economic crisis in the United States.

Wessel and Hantman, after balancing prices paid to producers against rising costs of agricultural inputs such as fertilizer and energy (oil), conclude that 'farmers and consumers have reaped *no* benefits from the export boom'.[5] Farm bankruptcies are near an all-time high, and the number of people working in agriculture has declined by 80 percent over the past forty years.

The current plight of farmers relying on exports is closely related to the structure of the marketing system, especially its secrecy, its concentration, and the accepted Western world practice of permitting private commodity and financial markets to gamble with the world's money and food supplies. In operations akin to those of a Las Vegas casino, traders hedge their sales or purchases through 'futures' trading and speculate on the rise or fall of the value of the dollar and other currencies.

The concentration and secrecy of these maneuvers is demonstrable: 85 percent of global commerce in grain is handled by just six companies: Cargill, Continental, Louis Dreyfus, Bunge and Born, Mitsui-Cook, and André Garnac. Of these, only Mitsui-Cook is publicly held, which means that the others, under current federal law, need not comply with the disclosure requirements of the Securities and Exchange Commission. Such corporations enjoy a number of benefits. For example, they may –

- Operate through subsidiaries located in places far from American growing fields, such as Panama or Switzerland, with attendant tax benefits.
- Manipulate the timing of their transactions to maximize profits.
- Charge U.S. taxpayers for storage and shipping of commodities.

● Utilize unverifiable shipping destinations to avoid accountability.
● Buy or sell the currencies of the nations with which they deal, timing such transactions for maximum profit. To avoid taxes, these transactions may be handled through 'off shore' banks in such financial havens as the Cayman Islands or the Bahamas.

The objective, as Gilmore puts it simply, 'is to purchase grain supplies at the lowest possible price in a highly competitive market in order to sell in a market that they virtually dominate.'[6]

Volume, to these traders, is at least as important as price, and sometimes more so. They get their 'cut' on all shipments, over and above the control of prices paid to producers.

Even the largest American corporate farms are wary of challenging this oligopsony (i.e., a few buyers who dominate a market) by attempting to manage their own international trade. Some of the larger farm cooperatives are attempting to break into the magic circle, but so far are handling less than 10 percent of the grain export market.

Playing the subsidy game

If government and the big grain traders are the ruling gods of agricultural exports, then Public Law 480, also known as Food for Peace, is their prophet. It is largely due to the concessional, low-interest, long-term loans and outright grants which PL-480 provides that the U.S. became the world's largest grain exporter, providing in 1979-80 64 percent of the total trade and 68 percent of developing country imports.[7]

It is less well known that other programs dispense credit or give credit guarantees to foreign food buyers or U.S.

traders. Among the more important are those of the Export-Import Bank and the Commodity Credit Corporation (CCC). The latter plays a major role as buyer and seller of last resort for American producers, and therefore as the creditor of domestic agricultural price-support programs. However, in recent years CCC also has participated, as have other government lending agencies, in the arrangement of 'blended' export credits, utilizing combinations of federal loan guarantees and private sector capital. Even in 1977, when commercial rather than government-to-government sales accounted for 95 percent of total U.S. grain exports, PL-480 continued to play an important role in keeping U.S. commodity prices high at home but competitive in foreign markets.

Many developing countries first introduced to U.S. farm exports through 'Food for Peace' are now proudly described by U.S. government spokespersons as having 'graduated' to become commercial customers. South Korea and Taiwan are often cited as examples. This concept of 'graduation' from PL-480 can be misleading, however, for the supporting hand of Washington continues to be available to further private sales by other means. For instance, Agriculture Secretary John Block testified before Congress in April 1983 that the 'blended credit' route was utilized in 1982 to finance the export sale of more than seven million tons of U.S. agricultural products.[8] These included wheat and wheat flour, corn, rice, cotton, soybeans and meal, tallow, tobacco, vegetable oil, and other commodities. According to the Secretary, another deal involved what he called 'creative use of CCC credit guarantees,' whereby American millers were 'awarded' U.S. government-owned wheat, which helped them to bid successfully on a contract to sell flour to Egypt.

It would have been politically hazardous for Congress to curtail benefits to farmers in the 1984 election year. Not surprisingly therefore, expansion of the PL-480 program and additional direct export credits and loan guarantees were included in a 'grab-bag' farm bill enacted in early

1984. An amendment authored by Democratic Senator John Melcher of Montana even added a new category of government export supports to encourage the sale and donation of surplus dairy products to needy nations. The exact amount of the FY 1985 increase for PL-480 was undecided as of late 1984, but the White House had recommended $118 million more in Title I (concessional food sales) for FY 1985. To the regret of private charitable organizations, no increase was proposed for Title II, which covers human needs-oriented grants.

Most U.S. farmers join the traders in praising such government export support devices, apparently assuming that their interests coincide. To the contrary, the trader is the biggest winner, and at lesser risk. The grain companies do not depend for their profits on escalating prices, but rather on inside information which allows them to predict market shifts either up or down. Such informed speculation allows the companies to make money whatever direction prices may move in, a game plan which is unavailable to all but the largest producers.

Private manipulation of world food markets by these means contradicts and undermines the three Congressionally stated objectives of PL-480 legislation, which are: 'To spur economic development within recipient countries, to develop markets for U.S. agricultural commodities and to promote U.S. foreign policy objectives.' Foreign markets 'developed' on the basis of outright donations or publicly financed credit are artificial constructs rather than true business transactions. Moreover, the foreign policy goals they presumably promote can be destructive or immoral as demonstrated for nearly a generation in the case of Vietnam and Iran, and more recently through the economic support generously doled out to Latin American dictatorships more intent on the suppression than the economic well-being of their people.

The Presidential Hunger Commission of 1980 was well aware of these distortions of the law's intent, and warned that it 'is too easily subverted by short term foreign policy considerations.' The Commission also opposed the use of food aid as a weapon, through the practice of granting it only to countries considered friendly, 'thereby denying food to innocent people when they are in greatest need.'[9] The Reagan Administration's selective use of these programs as both carrot and stick in Central America demonstrates the extent to which the Commission's advice has been ignored.

The chickens come home to roost

The export dependence generated by years of massive government subsidies and further stimulated by huge grain sales to the Soviet Union during the early 1970s shows no sign of decline, although our market share is shrinking. The 1982 and 1983 downturn in farm exports reflected both the global recession and a rapid increase in competition for Third World markets, notably from members of the ten-nation European Community (EC). The over-valued U.S. dollar, contributing to higher prices for buyers of American products, and escalating LDC debts made matters worse. The occasional shipment of dirty grain to foreign customers may be another factor contributing to the recent loss of the U.S. competitive edge. The Soviet Union complained about this in November 1984, and there had been previous criticism from other foreign customers as well as by U.S. observers.

Discussing one such cargo, Gordon Fraser, former U.S. agricultural attaché in Indonesia, remarked publicly: 'While the prevalence of weevils was not to the extent that the bags appeared to be moving, that probably would have been the case in a few more days.'[10] William Rodman, who served as a U.S. agricultural attaché in London, has been quoted by George Kohl, Washington-based development economist, thus: 'To say they [the customers] are perturbed is the understatement of the year. In brief, they state that too often they do not receive what they order and pay for, that they apparently do not have redress to their problems, and that if a solution cannot be found their orders will go elsewhere.'[11]

The United States, in short, is no longer cock of the walk in the agricultural export business.

Under the protection of its Common Agricultural Policy, the EC's share of world food exports of all kinds increased from 8.3 percent in 1976 to 18.3 percent in 1981, while the U.S. average share remained level at about 18 percent.[12] As early as 1975, the then Secretary of Agriculture, Earl Butz, felt impelled to declare war on the barriers protecting the EC's internal markets from U.S. agricultural imports, but the challenge is growing. For instance, EC wheat exports reached one-third of our own by 1982, up from one-seventh in 1977.

Retaliation and its attendant resentments are in the wind. Thomas Graham, former deputy general counsel in the Office of the U.S. Trade Representative, warned in 1983: 'The White House is ready to unload huge agricultural stockpiles on foreign markets in retaliation against West European export subsidies that push U.S. farm products out of those markets.'[13] He noted that there also are rising threats from other producer nations and that these are pushing the Reagan Administration and Congress toward protectionism as a counter-measure. One possibility, Graham writes, is that 'America will soon drop past trade preferences for advanced developing countries, including Brazil and Mexico.' The Administration has since announced that the list will also include Taiwan, Hong Kong and South Korea.

The U.S. soybean industry is keeping an especially watchful eye on Brazil, where Cargill and other producer-processors are currently developing soybean processing plants in direct competition with the U.S. Another source of concern for U.S. growers is Japan's continuing resistance to U.S. attempts to sell more beef and citrus fruits there. From the same side of the world, New Zealand's Prime Minister Robert Muldoon in 1984 expressed his concern to

President Reagan that the United States might 'dump' large quantities of surplus dairy products on the market. New Zealand is heavily dependent on dairy exports, as are several of the EC countries.

Some agricultural specialists in Congress and the Administration believe a worldwide era of protectionism and increasingly aggressive marketing practices has now begun. For the United States, this may mean abandonment of a long history of 'free trade' advocacy in favor of product-for-product bilateral agreements and strict reciprocity. This policy has a powerful supporter in the person of Republican Senator John Danforth of Missouri, chairman of the Senate's Subcommittee on International Trade, who has proposed legislation requiring other countries to grant the same access to U.S. goods as the U.S. grants theirs.

If these views continue to gain influence, the General System of Preferences may become politically difficult for Congress. Under the GSP the U.S. grants duty-free entry to some 140 countries, and 2,900 products, but its opponents say most of the benefits go to newly industrialized countries which do not need them.

Members of Congress who fear foreign competition have also attempted to further curtail the Reagan Administration's already watered-down Caribbean Basin Initiative by exempting certain products of these tiny nations from import preferences where they compete with American-produced foods. Sugar, beef and veal are among the Caribbean products under scrutiny.

Another result of creeping bilateralism may be declining influence for the eighty-eight member nation General Agreement on Tariffs and Trade (GATT), which has been weakened as an arbiter of international trade by the current epidemic of protectionism. U.S. attempts to protect its foreign agricultural markets from European competitors during the 1974-79 'Tokyo Round' of GATT negotiations got nowhere, as the EC continued to insist that it has shared equally with America in filling the growing world demand for food.

Many U.S. politicians appear to understand that such escalating competition is to be expected in view of the growth of the export capacities of other countries. They also recognize the need to continue the GSP system for poorer countries which need to export to pay their mounting debts. However, the pressure from constituents for continuing and tightening import restrictions is enormous.

Such issues have created a free-for-all among lobbyists and legislators. Preliminary skirmishing began in March 1984 when Democratic Representative James H. Weaver of Oregon, considered something of a maverick by big agribusiness interests, suggested an Export Grain Bank that would set an official price for some U.S. exported commodities, particularly grains. Free market advocates turned thumbs down on the proposal, although it is hardly revolutionary. Canada and several other major exporting nations already handle sales through government boards or government-ordered price ceilings. The idea has not yet been revived in the 99th Congress. Its prospects will not be good while farm bloc and business interests continue to reject out of hand any semblance of federal manipulation or regulation of price mechanisms beyond those (such as PL-480) which can be counted on to increase rather than curb the volume of their business and/or the level of their earnings.

Curiously, these U.S. government and private sector objections to government interference in the world food trade do not always extend to the formation of inter-nation trader cartels, particularly at times when protection is needed against falling prices. This double vision has been exhibited in the case of the wheat trade through periodic attempts by the U.S. to persuade major producing countries to act in concert. Gilmore notes that the U.S. has consistently sought to bring the European Community 'into conformity with uniform international guidelines regarding export price levels and marketing.'[14] However, the EC has held out for links between such an agreement and other outstanding trade issues, such as acceptance of its own protectionist agricultural policies.

The U.S. also appealed to other exporters to withhold grain supplies from the U.S.S.R. when Washington put an embargo on such sales in 1980, but the attempt was largely ignored by Argentina and Brazil, who used the U.S. embargo as an opportunity to increase their own exports to the Soviets at premium prices.

Attempts to allocate markets under the so-called International Wheat Agreements, first attempted shortly after World War II and since sporadically renegotiated, have also been systematically emasculated by governments and traders alike. However, there is strong belief in Congress and the grain industry that if surpluses continue to be difficult and expensive to get rid of, the U.S. may drop its current free market rhetoric in favor of attempting to negotiate binding market controls among major Western world producers.

If such official conventions fail to materialize, new attempts at pursuing the private cartel route are expected. Gilmore takes the position that 'neither option is extremely promising as long as the U.S. and other countries fail to deal with domestic production and distribution issues, which are equally relevant to the problems of food security and price stabilization.' He adds: 'An international agreement can at best provide a conducive setting but only participating members can guarantee effective results.'[15]

The Third World: winners and losers

The question of whether U.S. agricultural trade and aid has done the less-developed countries (as distinct from First World traders) more harm than good is highly controversial, and answers tend to vary according to the perceived interests of the beholder. However, the weight of evidence now in strongly suggests that while such assistance has provided some short-term benefits, it also is doing much long-range harm.

On the positive side, U.S. food shipments have fed millions of the world's poorest of the poor who otherwise would undoubtedly have died of starvation. Millions of children have been spared the tragic effects of chronic malnutrition and its attendant diseases, although such efforts have been too little and too late, particularly in famine-ravaged Africa. Food aid in times of drought, earthquakes and other natural disasters also has saved many lives. Distribution programs conducted through responsible charitable, often church-affiliated, organizations have generally been the most helpful. These private volunteer organizations (PVOs) distribute much of the food exported under Title II of PL-480, which authorizes outright grants of U.S. farm products to the poorest nations. However, many of the PVOs have been consistent critics of food shipments under Title I (concessional sales) because they believe there is inadequate supervision of food distribution by consignees.

Looked at from this viewpoint, the issue of cost versus benefits is complicated by the differing policies of recipient governments, and by differences of interest between ruling elites and the poor. Corruption, inefficiency, waste and private profiteering have been endemic in the distribution of American aid within many LDCs, especially within government-to-government and private commercial programs. Food intended for donation to the poor has been diverted to commercial channels, and LDC traders have jacked up prices to the point where the neediest people find it impossible to buy the grain or other products provided. In addition, much spoilage has resulted from carelessness or the absence of suitable storage and transport facilities.

In his book *Against the Grain*, Tony Jackson of Oxfam-Britain estimates that more than 70 percent of food sold to the LDCs is used by recipient governments to support their budgets, rather than for humanitarian purposes. He adds that governments often sell these imports to those who can afford them and use the proceeds as they like. For these reasons, among others, Jackson concludes that free handouts of food do not address the poverty program – they aggravate it.[16]

Ward Sinclair, agricultural writer for the *Washington Post*, has expressed the similar view that, contrary to popular belief, U.S. farmers are not 'feeding the world's hungry.' The bulk of the exports, he writes, go to countries that could pay cash, and most of the grain is used for animal feed.[17] The poor, of course, cannot afford to buy the meat produced with this grain.

Corruption and waste unfortunately are only the tip of the food aid iceberg. More intractable and potent dangers lie in wait over the long haul for poor countries which use such ostensible largesse unwisely. Among the most ominous of these is the creeping destruction of agricultural self-reliance. Many LDC governments, if subjected to outside prodding in support of inside reforms, could put their poor people in a position to grow their own food or to earn enough through urban employment to buy local produce.

This is not to say that U.S. food shipments to the Third World could be now safely cut off. According to a report by the Transnational Institute: 'In 1985 the developing market economy countries will have a net cereal deficit of almost 85 million tons compared with "only" 16 million tons annual average between 1969-1971'[18]

Some of this growing deficit is due to population growth. At the time of Christ the population of the world was about 300 million. In 1980 it was 4.3 billion, multiplying fourteen times in 2,000 years. World population now doubles in thirty-seven years.[19] Surely the world will need an ever-increasing supply of food to feed these billions, but just as surely more effective programs than those now in progress must be found to reduce birth rates.

On the other hand, food deficit countries could do much more than they are now doing to expand production for domestic consumption. The Independent Commission on International Development Issues, chaired by former West German Chancellor Willy Brandt, has estimated that one-half of 1 percent of one year's military spending in the world would buy all of the farm equipment needed to increase food production and approach food sufficiency by 1990.[20] However, many Third World governments much prefer to accept food aid, rather than undertake the politically explosive land reforms which will be necessary if their rural populations are to feed themselves. Such governments are also more likely to spend what foreign exchange they may earn from their own exports on military equipment or luxury goods rather than on bread for their people. Moreover, 'bargain' imports of U.S. food have the unhealthy side-effect of reducing the marketability of locally grown foodstuffs, driving prices below subsistence levels for small farmers.

The Carter Administration Hunger Commission did not pull any punches in discussing these evils of American food aid programs:

> At best, there is an inherent contradiction between food aid, which increases the dependency of recipients upon donors, and measures to increase purchasing power and basic food production within the developing countries themselves. . . . In some cases food aid undermines the efforts of recipient nations to develop a more self-reliant agricultural base of their own. Food aid has also enabled some recipient governments to postpone essential agricultural reforms, to give low priority to agricultural investment, and to maintain a pricing system which gives farmers inadequate incentives to increase local production.[21]

The twenty-member Commission, politically bipartisan and including members from both houses of Congress, as well as strong representation from the agribusiness community, universities and the public, showed the PL-480 program in its present form little mercy. It concluded that 'the interests of farmers and exporters would be better served if market development were reduced or even eliminated as an objective of the food aid program,' and recommended that 'Congress undertake a complete revision of the PL-480 Food for Peace program to enable the program to accord more closely with the New Directions approach to development assistance.'[22] ('New Directions' is a phrase first used by Congress in 1973 foreign aid legislation instructing the Administration to focus its assistance more closely on meeting the basic human needs of the Third World's poor.)

So far Congress has not undertaken any such reform of PL-480. However, a number of human needs-oriented, non-profit organizations in 1983 supported a 'Land for Food' amendment to existing aid legislation to try and ensure that more agricultural land in the Caribbean Basin countries would produce food for local use. Another promising Congressional initiative was the Human Needs and World Security Act introduced in the House in late 1983 with forty-two co-sponsors. The broad purpose of the Act was to create a better balance than now exists between genuine development programs and those devoted to military and security assistance. It also would have increased current appropriations for the International Fund for Agricultural Development, which gives technical aid to small LDC farmers, and for emergency food aid to drought-stricken sub-Sahara African countries. Neither piece of legislation passed.

'Export cropping' and U.S. investment

U.S. agricultural export promotion programs have been linked ingeniously by Congress to American private sector investment in the Third World. For example, the now-dormant 'Cooley loan' program (named after the North Carolina representative who devised the scheme in 1957) permitted American corporations to borrow the local currency generated by the sale of PL-480 financed products in recipient countries. This money, available for local invest-ment, was eagerly snapped up, and many foreign oper-ations so financed continue to prosper. According to the San Francisco-based Institute for Food and Development Policy, the Cooley legislation has been used to help underwrite the establishment of 419 subdivisions of American firms in thirty-one Third World countries at very low cost. In India alone, such loans have been made to Wyeth Labs, Otis Elevator, Sylvania, Rockwell, Goodyear, CPC International, Sunshine Farms, First National City Bank of America and American Express, among others.[23] The loans were also used by major U.S. grain traders and agribusiness firms to help finance storage and processing plants in the LDCs.

Similar arrangements now can be made under different provisions of PL-480. These permit negotiation of agreements between the U.S. and LDC governments under which payment for certain Food for Peace products may be waived if the proceeds of local sale are used for agreed-upon development projects. Another current incentive for U.S. investors to take their money and jobs abroad to low-wage nations is the Caribbean Basin Initiative. This Reagan-inaugurated 'aid' program of import preferences and investment financing serves the tiny island nations of the area, as well as the 'friendly' countries of revolution-torn Central America along the basin's rim (Nicaragua and Cuba are excluded).

Worldwide, nearly $500 million from the sale of U.S. concessional food shipments has been used over the past twenty years to make loans at below-market interest rates to U.S. agribusiness firms for operations abroad.[24] Many of these firms are now competing with American farmers. For example, Del Monte, which made its original fortune in California, now grows tomatoes, peaches, apricots and pears in several foreign countries, including Italy, Greece and South Africa. ALCOSA, the Spanish acronym for a Guatemalan frozen food company owned by U.S. investors, supplies U.S. supermarkets with broccoli, cauliflower and okra.[25]

Such conflicts of interest between U.S. Agency for International Development (AID)-supported multinational agribusiness abroad and domestic agriculture have lurked in the corners of AID food programs for years. As early as

1977, Frances Moore Lappé and Joseph Collins of the Institute for Food and Development Policy reported in detail on the operations of the AID-backed Latin American Agribusiness Development Corporation (LAAD), an investment enterprise owned by fifteen U.S.-based parent companies. They found that LAAD, which has had projects in Central America, Colombia and Chile, among other locales, gave most of its money to 'luxury export operations such as beef, fresh and frozen vegetables, cut flowers and wood products. . . . Due to the increasing impoverishment of the majority of people in the countries where LAAD invests, the company was unable to sell locally what its associated firms produced . . . agricultural products then go to the highest bidders, notably in the United States.'[26]

Growing competition with U.S. agriculture probably can be expected from the LDCs in the years ahead, much of it financed at least in part by U.S. capital. According to a report by the General Accounting Office, an investigative arm of the Congress, Mexico in ten to twenty years could supply all of the fruits and vegetables consumed in the U.S. during winter.[27] Currently it provides 50 percent of the tomatoes consumed in the winter, and also provides large quantities of squash, eggplant, cucumbers, asparagus and broccoli. The low wages paid by Mexican growers (many of them subsidiaries of U.S. firms) provide the necessary competitive edge against U.S. domestic production and deprive American farmworkers of their livelihoods.

The Dominican Republic now exports 64 percent of its agricultural production, mostly sugar. Almost all of the production and the land on which the cane is grown is controlled by the U.S.-based multinational Gulf and Western Corporation. The country is plagued by severe malnutrition and miserable rural wages of less than $50 per month. These conditions spur migration to city slums, where unemployment runs at 25 percent.

This kind of U.S. government-stimulated foreign investment has stirred strong anxieties among organized

American workers, including farm labor. AFL-CIO President Lane Kirkland has warned that the duty-free entry provisions of the Caribbean Basin Initiative will cost a substantial number of jobs, even though over 80 percent of the products now produced in these countries already enter the U.S. duty-free under the General System of Preferences. Critics of the CBI also believe that increased U.S. agribusiness investment will not help the diets of the poor. They note that land now available for the production of local staples such as corn and beans is being diverted to the raising of beef for export to the U.S. and other affluent countries. The above-mentioned 'Land for Food' amendment to CBI legislation approved by Congress in 1983 attempts to avert such abuses by requiring the U.S. to withhold CBI trade concessions until governments agree to produce more food for home consumption. How strictly it will be enforced remains to be seen, since it provides for Presidential discretion in its application.

U.S. agriculture's collision course with Third World food production, spurred by American capital investment, is even more frightening than these examples suggest. As economist Michael Perelman has estimated: 'A little more than one-third of our agricultural exports are sent to Africa, Latin America and Asia, excluding Japan. In return these nations devote much of their land to producing crops for the U.S. . . . In 1971, the U.S. imported about $4 billion worth of agricultural products from Africa, Latin America and Asia, excluding Japan. By 1975, this amount had grown by 63 percent to more than $6 billion.'[28]

This was a period in which U.S. farm exports, thanks to government props such as PL-480, grew at an even faster rate than they are doing now. However, as we have seen, these sales started to decline in the early 1980s. Meanwhile, the competition from Third World governments for expanded foreign outlets for both their farm and manufactured products continues to grow. In 1950 U.S. producers enjoyed a $12 billion export surplus. In 1983 imports of manufactured goods exceeded exports by $38 billion.

What the Third World needs – and what it gets

The complaints of Third World nations against what they perceive to be unfair treatment by the more affluent market economy countries (often called the North-South conflict) were given a strong organizational base and explicit documentation following the March 1964 establishment in Geneva of the United Nations Conference on Trade and Development (UNCTAD). This organization has become the forum in which the original 'Group of Seventy-Seven' LDCs – now numbering more than a hundred – formulated their demands for a New International Economic Order (NIEO).

One of this group's bitterest grievances has been the disparity between the prices it must pay for agricultural and manufactured goods from the North, as opposed to those it receives for its own exports. These exports, despite LDC industrial growth, continue in most cases to be predominantly unprocessed raw materials, both mineral and agricultural. In agriculture, the occupation for over half of the people in LDCs, statistics are revealing: in 1960, for instance, twenty-five tons of Sri Lanka's natural rubber would buy six farm tractors, but by 1980 it would purchase less than two.

To correct this situation, the South has proposed a number of remedies, including the following:

- A global 'redistribution of income.' The 1976 UNCTAD Conference in Nairobi called on the advanced capitalist countries to give 0.7 percent rather than the present 0.35 percent of their gross national products to foreign aid.[29] (Excluding the oil-producing countries, the South has three-fourths of the world's population, but only one-fourth of its income.)
- The negotiation of 'commodity agreements' to stabilize world prices for the South's agricultural and mineral exports, and indexing of these prices to those paid for imports from the North.

- Reform of international financial institutions such as the World Bank and International Monetary Fund to put them on a one-nation-one-vote basis. At present, voting is weighted according to the capital contributions of member countries. At present, the U.S. alone casts 23 percent of the votes in the IMF and World Bank. LDC governments willing to curtail social benefits for their people often appear to be favored borrowers.

- Easier access to the North's markets for the growing variety of goods produced by the South, through the reduction of tariff and non-tariff trade barriers. The South particularly resents industrial nations' insistence on doing their own processing of imported raw materials. For instance, the tiny country of Guyana on the Caribbean rim has long complained that multinational firms which buy its sugar demand it raw and do the refining in other countries.

So far the South has not done very well in trying to persuade the North to meet its demands. For example:

- The 'Integrated Program for Commodities' inaugurated under UNCTAD auspices in 1974 has not gotten off the ground. Its most important provision is for a so-called Common Fund to finance the purchase of buffer stocks of LDC commodities in times of surplus and to sell them in times of scarcity. Designed to stabilize world market prices, the Fund is now seeking a modest contribution from member countries of about $750 million, although Third World nations originally hoped to collect $3-$6 billion. The U.S. has yet to make a donation, and buffer stocks have not been established for any of the international commodity agreements currently in effect. The sugar and coffee agreements as presently written are not eligible for Fund coverage, and the buffer provisions for cocoa are not functioning. Supporters of the program hope that a more sympathetic Administration and Congress would help put the program in operation.

- The idea of dropping weighted voting in the multi-lateral lending institutions is not regarded as realistic in either U.S. or most Western European financial circles.

- Foreign aid of the type which contributes to genuine human development in the Third World – that which helps to raise living standards of the poor and contributes to their self-reliance – has been very much out of style with the Reagan Administration. On the other hand, military and 'security' assistance, including 'economic support funds' for strategically located friendly governments, has prospered. As noted, legislation to bring about a better balance between development and security assistance was introduced in the House at the end of the 1983 session, and for the first time during the Reagan Administration Congress approved, for FY 1985, a larger increase in development aid than it did for the military security variety of foreign assistance – although the shift was not of major proportions. People-oriented AID development programs directed toward meeting human needs under the Reagan budget for FY 1985 were funded at $1.4 billion, a minute increase from the $1.3 billion for FY 1984. On the other hand, almost $14 billion had been requested for FY 1985 for various military and security-related programs. Israel, Egypt and 'friendly' Central American countries were the chief beneficiaries of this type of assistance.

- Easier access to U.S. markets for LDC goods is likely to be difficult to achieve on any large scale in the immediate future. Protectionist sentiment, as previously noted, is on the rise, and the U.S. is buying most of its imports from a small number of countries. The Hunger Commission found that 70 percent of goods now imported into the U.S. under GSP agreements originate in just five countries: Brazil,

Taiwan, South Korea, Mexico and Hong Kong.[30]
According to the Commission, a further difficulty is
that demand for non-oil primary commodities has
grown only slowly in recent years, the purchasing
power of the U.S. and some other industrial countries
has declined, and prices of LDC products are very
erratic. Moreover, for exportable foodstuffs many
LDCs are confined to a very narrow range of 'core
commodities,' such as coffee, tropical fruits, cocoa,
etc. The American market for Latin American-grown
vegetables, however, appears to be growing.

Aside from purchases of relatively few such products,
U.S. food traders remain basically export–rather than
import–oriented, and our foreign aid programs, reflecting
commercial fears of 'losing' Third World food markets,
have done relatively little to help the LDCs feed themselves. Secretary of Agriculture John Block told the House
Agriculture and Foreign Affairs Committees in April 1983:
'It concerns me that there seems to be a tendency in some
countries around the world to produce farm commodities
under very uneconomic conditions, and the justification
being that they want self-sufficiency. Of course, there are
political and social reasons also, but we should not be part
of that kind of game.'[31]

The global food security paradox

Starvation and malnutrition among the world's people is
caused not by lack of resources to feed them, but by the
absence of the political will to do so. These conclusions are
shared by the U.S. General Accounting Office. In a 1980
report, the GAO determined that 'private interests,
national economies, the world food economy and the world
economy in general, as currently managed, rely in a major
way on the continued existence of a large, poor, rural
peasantry.' It also makes the direct charge that 'some

governments are uninterested in increasing food production or simply do not want the rural poor to benefit from these efforts.'[32]

The U.S. agribusiness complex, with its far-flung foreign subsidiaries, cannot be counted on to be of great assistance in this situation. The Presidential Hunger Commission reported that 'neither corporations nor developing countries see much of a role for foreign private investment in direct efforts to alleviate hunger and malnutrition among the very poor. Agribusiness executives themselves are virtually unanimous in recognizing the limitations of their own organizations in meeting these particular needs.'[33]

It appears, then, that more foreign markets for U.S. export agriculture and U.S. investment in food production abroad are not expected or intended to cure world hunger. Although admirable catch-phrases, neither 'trade *and* aid' nor 'trade *not* aid' is an effective tool for this purpose, as now practiced. Where then are solutions to be sought?

'Food security' for most of the world's 4.7 billion people is widely conceived to be theoretically possible at present, but only if more equitable means of distributing nutriments and the land they are grown on are enforced. Unfortunately, it seems unlikely that this will occur on any large scale in the foreseeable future. Moreover, if global population growth continues at its present rate of about 82 million a year, even a massive redistribution and reorganization of world agriculture would not suffice. Nevertheless, there are a few good omens discernible on the trade and hunger horizon, although some of them must be carefully hedged. For instance:

● A 'population crisis' is not inevitable. When living
   standards improve, population growth tends to slow
   up. Richard Barnet points out that there is a
   relationship between the level of prosperity of a
   country and its birth rate, provided that prosperity is
   decently distributed. In an acerbic reference to the
   U.S. government's birth control programs in the Third

World, he notes that we do not know nearly enough about the relationship between social economic and cultural policies and human reproduction, 'but we know enough to recognize that birth rates respond much less to propaganda and bombardment by condoms than to equitable economic and social policies.'[34]

- It is well within the realm of political and economic realism to enhance the world's reserve stocks of food, particularly grains, against times of famine or shortages, and to see to it that they are more equitably distributed by recipient countries. Internationally controlled organizations such as the U.N. Food and Agriculture Organization and the World Food Council already exist for these purposes. Similar programs are available for assisting farmers in the LDCs to produce more food for family consumption and for the millions now flooding Third World cities in search of industrial work. Unfortunately, the U.S. must bear a considerable share of the responsibility for the failure of these efforts so far to realize their full potential. Every administration in Washington since World War II has been miserly with projects conducted through the United Nations and its specialized agencies, preferring bilateral programs which are easier to control.

- The U.S. now maintains a security reserve of four million metric tons of wheat, which is isolated from the market under current law. In addition, some of the LDCs are now setting aside national reserves of their own. However, U.S. farmers traditionally have opposed reserve programs for fear the government might use them to hold down prices. One result of this distrust, according to Gilmore, has been that 'at no time has the U.S. tried to fashion a [reserve] program that would integrate domestic and international concerns' – despite the fact that USDA projections showed world grain carry-over stocks falling from 16.7 percent of world utilization in July 1983 to 11.7 percent by July 1984.[35] Most of the reduction was expected to be due to a large drop in corn production. However, wheat, the primary world food import, was expected to be in over supply.

The U.S. has been wary of many international programs, including the World Food Council (WFC), the International Fund for Agricultural Development (IFAD) and the Food Security Assistance Scheme (FSAS), the latter a project of the United Nations Food and Agriculture Organization (FAO). According to the General Accounting Office, the federal government has had difficulty identifying suitable projects in the LDCs for resources allocated to the WFC.[36] On the other hand, ministers of agriculture and other officials representing seventy-three countries who attended the WFC's 1983 meeting warned that during the last decade thirty-seven developing countries – including twenty-three out of forty-two African countries – have had negative growth rates in per capita grain production. Obviously the search for 'suitable projects' needs to be more serious.

In 1984, the widely respected Washington-based ecumenical religious organization Interfaith Action for Economic Justice took the position that U.S. support for IFAD has been 'lukewarm' and 'has forced that organization to cut back by one-third its lending for projects benefiting small farmers and landless laborers. . . . The [Reagan] Administration's request for $50 million for IFAD in FY/85 would leave IFAD still $40 million short of what is needed to complete the U.S. contribution to the first replenishment, already a year overdue.'[37]

The Food Security Assistance Scheme, on its part, has provided financial and technical assistance to about twenty low-income, food-deficit countries and is the primary UN mechanism for the receipt of donations for development from the Organization of Petroleum Exporting Countries (OPEC). However, the United States, although a member, has yet to appropriate funds for it. Most of the contributions so far have come from the Scandinavian countries.

The 'South-South trade' solution is offered as an ultimate avenue of hope for the developing countries in their peoples' efforts (not always shared fully by their governments) to become reasonably self-reliant in food production and less dependent on the debt-enhancing unreliable export push of the First World. Their aspiration is to buy and sell more from each other, and this type of reciprocal trade is increasing. The customers exist, and means for financing them will be found. Leadership in this effort is devolving naturally on a few of the more industrialized LDCs, such as Brazil, South Korea and Taiwan. Brazil is already a formidable exporter of grains to Third World markets, and has sold commercial aircraft to Nigeria. India is exporting sugar to Egypt, bicycle parts to Uganda, hand tools to Iraq and finished leather to Iran.

The second report of the Brandt Commission on International Development discusses this phenomenon in detail, concluding: 'The possibility of low growth rates and of continuing protection in the developed countries increases the need for such [South-South] cooperation.' The Commission also sees possibilities in expanded regional cooperation among even the poorer LDCs, and sees promising developments in this direction in Western and Southern Africa, as well as within the Caribbean community.[38]

Third World nations are now probing many such avenues in their attempts to diminish dependence on expensive loans and often unrewarding trade or investment forays by the industrial countries. It is unfortunate that in this search the plight of the poor and the hungry is often considered of secondary importance to protecting the interests of business and government elites. Increasingly, however, the disadvantaged classes are challenging further exploitation, whatever the source, by political means if possible, by revolution if all else fails. The violent phase of the process is already well under way in Central America, Africa and parts of Asia.

A desperate search for food and the land on which to

grow it, or for jobs and income with which to buy it, is under way, and the affluent societies can expect to feel the backlash – a bit of handwriting on the wall which the specialists of the U.S. General Accounting Office have read also, much more clearly than their employers on Capitol Hill. Social and economic deterioration within the less-developed world, the GAO warns, can be translated to the richer countries through the depression of trade. Therefore, explains the GAO, 'continued impoverishment of the world's rural peasantry, while serving relatively limited private interests, is economically disadvantageous to majorities in poor and rich countries alike.'[39]

Ultimately, the national security of the United States and other Western industrial societies will depend on their ability to find peaceful, equitable solutions to these problems of world hunger and world trade. President John F. Kennedy said it best in his 1961 Inaugural Address: 'If a free society cannot help the many who are poor, it cannot save the few who are rich.'

New directions

• Congress should completely revise PL-480. U.S. food aid should be specifically targeted to meet the needs of the poorest people in poor countries. Present emphasis in the program as a tool of market development should be eliminated, and its use as a political weapon through existing 'friendly countries only' criteria should be prohibited. Food aid agreements with the LDCs should be tightly worded to require that recipient governments take measures to increase their self-reliance in food production and reduce dependence on 'handouts.' Recipient governments should also be authorized to use the proceeds of the sale of PL-480 shipments to support the prices of home-grown food for local consumption. Implementation of effective land reform programs by governments receiving such assistance should also be required.

In the U.S., the time has come to put brakes on the mania for expanding agricultural exports at public expense. Untargeted and politically motivated government price-support programs have contributed to concentration of land ownership, soil depletion and rising costs of production inputs such as water, petroleum products and pesticides. They have also discouraged innovation and competition, while contributing to the demise of family-size farms. Poor Americans could make good use of much of the country's alleged agricultural 'over-production,' if they could afford to buy it.

● U.S. commodities markets and grain trading companies should be made more accountable to the public, and particularly to farmers. Accurate, timely market information should be guaranteed to producers by law. Secrecy is much prized by traders, who have their own information networks, but farmers and consumers have suffered from the food export boom in part because they lack these advantages and thus are at the traders' mercy. Reasonable price stability is also required by farmers in order to plan production intelligently. The trading companies, on the other hand, thrive on price instability because inside information permits them to gamble (usually successfully) on market fluctuations. A start should be made toward solving both the information and stability problems by tightening current regulations governing the floating crap game called speculation in the futures markets.

One method of doing this would be to increase the resources and authority of the Commodities Futures Trading Commission. For example, the Commission should be empowered to prevent companies from buying more of a commodity than needed to meet sales commitments. Price stability would also be encouraged by the introduction of an international grain reserve, a device which the government, under pressure from the traders' lobby, has traditionally opposed. (The Food Security Reserve program established in 1981 is inadequate for this purpose, being designed primarily to backstop PL-480 by holding supplies and making them available in times of shortage, when food aid programs would otherwise be cut back.) Congress should seriously consider the creation of an Export Grain Bank to set an official export price for some U.S. foods, particularly grains.

• The so-called Human Needs and World Security Act introduced in Congress at the end of 1983 was only a slight improvement over the longstanding and continuing 'tilt' in favor of security-related foreign aid programs. However, the balance needs to be further redressed in favor of genuine development projects specifically targeted to reduce world hunger and poverty. The practice of including in such legislation language which puts desirable reforms at the mercy of the President's discretion should be discontinued. The November 1983 proposals of the Reagan-appointed Commission on Security and Economic Assistance (the Carlucci Commission) to increase military and security-related foreign aid were especially unhealthy (although, as noted above, the balance between these types of support and development assistance were somewhat addressed for FY 1985). Such assistance should be frozen at 1984 levels or lower, and additional funds appropriated for new and innovative approaches to Third World development. Of special importance are projects which encourage self-reliant food production for local consumption and expand participation by the poor in raising their own living standards. In this respect, locally controlled community activities are more desirable than grandiose national plans to expand economic growth by such devices as subsidies or guarantees of investment by multinational corporations.

An excellent scenario for constructive, new-model anti-poverty programs abroad has been put forward by Washington-based economic development consultant Guy Gran. He recommends that such projects be kept small and insulated as much as possible from interference by ruling elites. Initial leadership would come from specialists unconnected with any government, corporation or other 'world system' organ. Most projects would involve the use of private volunteer specialists or representatives of charitable agencies, including the educated youth of both First and Third World countries.[40]

• Congress acted in 1985 to renew Generalized System of Preferences (GSP) legislation but did not make its import tariff benefits more widely available to the poorest countries, which need them most. Most of these benefits now go to some fifteen of the more well-to-do LDCs, such as Taiwan and South Korea. At the same time, provisions should be included in the legislation requiring GSP beneficiaries to respect the human rights of their workers (including their right to organize) and to refrain from diverting land to the production of export crops when it is needed to grow food for domestic consumption. The current practice of encouraging U.S. agribusiness producers to use the poorest LDCs as 'plantations' for growing export crops destined for American consumption should be discouraged. An additional criterion for granting GSP privileges should be the willingness of LDC governments to use the proceeds of export sales for productive purposes, forgoing unjustifiable expenditures for luxury goods. Washington could also help persuade LDCs to exercise self-restraint in this area by being less generous in its provision of commercial export credits to U.S. cor-porations.

• In general, the Third World suffers in its relations with the industrial nations from adverse terms of trade, which require poor nations to pay more for what they buy than they receive for what they sell. One route to correcting this situation lies in strengthening the so-called 'Common Fund,' under which buffer stocks of LDC commodities such as coffee, sugar, tea, jute and olive oil are put on the market or taken off it in order to stabilize prices. The Fund was first proposed by the LDCs in 1974 and agreed on in 1980. However, it has not prospered, largely due to the reluctance of industrial importing countries, including the U.S., to finance it adequately. (While a long-term step toward increasing the equity of world trade, a strengthened

Fund probably would not be of much immediate help to the Third World's poor, since most of the benefits would be distributed to commodity traders.)

• Congress should continue support for the Select Committee on Hunger of the House of Representatives, first established in early 1983. This committee has, through its public hearings and staff work, played a valuable role in publicizing food issues, generating support for reform, and providing advice to those with the power to effect change directly. The formation of a similar body by the Senate should also be encouraged. The House committee owes its life to two years of work by concerned members and a coalition of some sixty private organizations. Although the panel does not have the authority to write legislation, it is empowered to prepare studies and make recommendations to standing committees on a wide range of bills dealing with foreign and domestic hunger issues, world trade, foreign aid and related questions. It is a potentially valuable addition to Congress and can help attract the attention of members to issues of critical importance to world peace, and also to U.S. security in its broadest, long-range manifestation.

6 Conclusions: Toward the year 2000

This book was for the most part researched and written before or during consideration of the omnibus farm and food legislation of 1985. The final chapter takes into account what occurred in that and other important legislation. Nineteen eighty-five was supposed to be a watershed year for farm policy, but what has instead occurred in most areas is a muddling through. There were some pluses and some minuses in the Food Security Act of 1985, but most of the issues and solutions proposed in this book and by other reformers remain on the table. The economic, environmental and nutritional problems were not fully addressed, nor were complete solutions adopted in 1985. In some areas, such as soil conservation, there were victories. The food stamp program won a slight restoration of benefits cut since 1981. But underlying crises remain. In Africa, many are still in danger of starvation. In the United States, we are about to embark on a potentially dangerous new course of genetic engineering. And also at home there is the crisis of farm incomes, leading not just to fore-closures but to depression, suicides and even murder in the countryside.

Completion of the farm bill, signed as a sort of holiday gift on December 23, 1985, seems to leave us no closer to solving most of the problems of agriculture. On balance the bill was a mix of good and bad. The challenge now is to build on successes while attempting to hold losses to a minimum. Unfortunately for many farmers it is probably too late. Ronald Reagan and the departed David Stockman and John Block have in substantial part won their crusade, begun in 1981, for a more 'market-oriented' farm policy. The rest of us will now have to face the consequences.

Farm issues and programs

The economic crisis affecting many farmers will in fact be made worse by the legislation, which lowered farm income by lowering both price and income supports. That is not a misprint; the bill actually reduced farm income in a period of already depressed farm returns. The structural problems in agriculture – the decline of the small and moderate-size farm – were given some attention in the new law and in the comprehensive tax reform bill passed by the House of Representatives in late 1985. But much more on this front could have been accomplished. Attempts to deal explicitly with structural trends – in ways that would help preserve family farms – were for the most part dropped as the bill proceeded through Congress.

The 1985 farm bill included two historic changes in the way agricultural programs have operated over the last half-century. For the first time, soil conservation practices have been made mandatory for receipt of farm price-support benefits. And also for the first time in a farm bill, price-support loan rates have actually been lowered rather than raised.

The best part of the farm bill was a revolutionary change in federal soil conservation programs. 'Cross-compliance,' long a theory, is now part of the law in a modified way. Price supports and other benefits will not be available to farmers who fail to adopt good conservation practices on fragile land. In addition, the bill created a 40 to 45 million acre conservation reserve which will both protect against soil losses and enhance farm prices by trimming production. Farmers will be paid for enrolling acreage in the reserve, but projections are these costs – of about $50 per acre – will be less than the costs of price-support benefits. The reserve will be phased in over five years, starting with at least a 5 million acre reserve in 1986 and increasing to between 40 and 45 million acres in 1990.

The 'sodbuster' portion of the law attempts to discourage the cultivation of fragile lands. Planting on highly erodible land or filling in of sensitive wetlands for agricultural use will cause a farmer to forfeit his or her right to price supports and other farm-program benefits until conservation practices are restored. A 'grandfather' provision exempts from this new restriction fragile land planted between 1981 and 1985. One shortcoming of the sodbuster law is that it allows farmers until 1995 to develop conservation plans on exempted land. This means that poor conservation practices in some instances may continue for another decade. But on balance the new soil program was a major victory for conservationist groups such as the American Farmland Trust.

The central issues in farm legislation have usually revolved around prices for agricultural commodities and the relationship of government programs to those prices. In the 1980s, farm income has been way down for many producers. Historically low incomes in recent years have led to loan delinquencies and farm foreclosures. This is a crisis which now threatens to spill over into the overall economy, where 22 million workers are employed in food and farm-related industries. But the 1985 farm bill seems to provide little help for the farmers who are in the most trouble. The debt and income crisis faced by many farmers will in fact be aggravated by the legislation, which lowers farm prices by reducing price-support loans. This comes immediately. Then target-price income subsidies will also fall, after a two-year freeze.

For 1985, the last year for which the old programs were still in force, price-support loans were $3.30 per bushel for wheat and $2.55 per bushel for corn. The new law lowered these levels to $3.00 in 1986 for wheat and $2.40 for corn.

In addition, the law gave the Secretary of Agriculture discretion to lower loan rates by another 20 percent. The Reagan Administration on January 13, 1986, announced such a further reduction – to $2.40 for wheat and $1.92 for corn. The Administration also announced that, to be eligible for price and income supports, farmers will be required to participate in an extensive acreage-retirement program.

Price-support loans for 1987 and future years are to be based upon a formula which follows recent average market prices, but further declines in the loan rate are limited to no more than 5 percent a year (plus the discretionary 20 percent).

This reduction in the loan rates – and later in income subsidies – will mean lower farm income in the near future. But government farm commodity programs will still cost a bundle – over $50 billion for three years according to Congressional projections, but closer to $70 billion according to some other analysts. In a terrible irony, this is the most expensive farm bill in history, but – by lowering price and income supports – it may still play a role in forcing as many as 10 percent of all farmers out of business over the next two years. The Chase and Wharton Econometrics firms project $10 to $15 billion in losses to private banks because of farm failures in the near future.[1] And these losses will come on top of the severe loan-delinquency problems now faced by the cooperative banks of the Farm Credit System (FCS), which hold about one-third of the nation's $216 billion agricultural debt. Many of the System's borrowers are now in trouble, posing a danger not just to agriculture but to the overall economy. Bail-out legislation, also signed in December 1985 but separate from the farm bill, set up a federal line of credit for FCS banks and reorganized the System to provide more federal regulation.

The lowering of price supports is based on the hope that falling U.S. crop prices will stimulate foreign demand and thus increase farm exports. That is supposed to take care of our chronic problem of overproduction and at the same time force farm prices – and thus incomes – up. Then there will magically be no more need for expensive government farm programs. This is of course that old song, umpteenth verse, of Reaganomics. We can, the theory goes, grow our way out of hard times.

In agricultural policy, expansion of farm exports has become almost a religious quest. But will this panacea work? Ward Sinclair of the *Washington Post* cites experts who say no.[2] Other countries have increasingly developed the capacity to meet more of their own food needs. For example, State Department analyst Dennis Avery points out in *Science* magazine that, between 1972 and 1982, the agricultural output of the less-developed countries grew by one-third. Over the same period, developed countries increased their farm output by 18 percent.[3] This means fewer export markets for our farmers. It may mean a more self-reliant world, if that increased production feeds hungry people.

The structural problems in agriculture – the decline of the small and moderate-size farm – were given some but not enough attention in the new law. Attempts to deal with structural trends were for the most part dropped as the bill proceeded through Congress. The most prominent examples were attempts to direct farm-price and income supports to not larger than family-size farms. This 'targeting' effort has been and remains a goal of reformers. Although it was not successful in the 1985 bill, targeting did receive more serious discussion than ever before.

Some important procedural reforms for the loan programs of the Farmers Home Administration did get through. For example, 25 percent of farm ownership and operating loans must go to 'limited-resource' farmers; repossessed inventory property held by Farmers Home must be sold or leased to operators of not larger than family-size; foreclosed borrowers may lease back their farm homes and a small number of acres for up to five years; and, until there is a formal foreclosure, the agency must release to a borrower some farm receipts for necessary living and farm-operating expenses. Many of these reforms had been pushed by the Center for Rural Affairs and the Rural Coalition. The loss in the credit area was that the farm bill shifts large amounts of money from direct lending by Farmers Home to guaranteed lending by private banks. The government guarantees the private loans, but the procedural reforms in the 1985 bill apply only to direct loans.

Nineteen eighty-five was also a year of tax reform, touted by President Reagan as the leading domestic priority of his second term. To the President's credit, his original tax-reform proposals included several excellent changes in the tax code's impact on family farmers. Some of these reforms found a place in the final House-passed bill. That bill goes to the Senate for consideration in 1986. The most positive changes for family-farm agriculture in the House bill were elimination of the investment tax credit and changes in the depreciation schedules for certain expenditures. The bill changed the depreciation period from five to thirteen years for buildings used for livestock confinement, dairy and poultry. Stretching out that brief five-year period and ending the investment credit will make agriculture less attractive to non-farmer investors seeking tax shelters.

Food stamps

The food assistance title of the 1985 farm bill increased food stamp program benefits by a very modest $381 million. This increase will come over fiscal years 1986 to 1989. It is better than a further reduction, but the increase amounts to only about a 5 percent restoration in the $7 billion of food stamp budget cuts made during fiscal years 1982 through 1985.

The bill also authorized expanded work requirements for food stamp households. By April 1, 1987, all states will be required to have in place 'employment and training' programs in which a set percentage of food stamp households must participate. Some 'workfare' programs have been criticized for creating busywork and for providing no real transition to permanent employment. The budget savings in such programs often come from simply forcing people off the assistance rolls through bureaucratic confusion and barriers.

The specific benefit increases in the 1985 law were not in the form of an across-the-board raise for all food stamp recipients. The food stamp basic benefit allotment is based on the Thrifty Food Plan (see Chapter 4), but the Congress in earlier legislation already restored the benefit allotment to 100 percent of the Thrifty Food Plan. Changes in the 1985 farm legislation increased benefits for certain types of recipient households, most notably the working poor and the recently unemployed. This category of the unemployed includes farm households experiencing hard times.

Ironically, the one significant benefit cut in the bill affected recipients participating in on-the-job training (OJT) programs under the federal Job Training Partnership Act. Earnings from OJT programs now will be counted as income for food stamp purposes. This creates a major disincentive for the very poor to participate in these programs.

International food aid

The venerable Public Law 480, now in its thirty-second year of providing grants and concessional sales of U.S. farm products to the less developed countries, was revised in the Food Security Act to increase substantially shipments made either as outright gifts or as sales on below-market terms. However, the changes fell far short of the complete overhaul proposed by humanitarian and non-profit organizations. The new terms were part of the same export-promotion package that includes the farm price-support reductions mentioned above.

The P.L. 480 changes were straightforwardly intended to entice poor countries to accept more American exports. For example, concessional sales of farm products (Title I) may once again be paid for in foreign currencies rather than dollars, an attractive bait which had been disallowed for several years. The proceeds of these sales may be recycled as loans to banks and other financial institutions for undefined 'productive investment,' including the promotion of further U.S. commodity sales, or for 'self-help' farm programs in eligible countries. The catch is that the private sector will be the favored recipient of these funds. Publicly-financed programs were specifically ruled out. Moreover, the Third World is left with little incentive to stabilize or increase the prices paid its own farmers for domestic food production. Some governments also may be drawn into the inflationary temptation of merely printing the local currency needed to buy Title I food.

The farm bill authorized increases in minimum tonnages of donated food (Title II), but this too may do more long-term harm than good in some food-short nations. Lower priority is given to the expansion of local production, and as 'gift' shipments are increased so are opportunities for fraud and mismanagement in distribution by foreign governments. Despite the dedicated efforts of American private relief organizations to prevent them, these are problems which have plagued P.L. 480 since its beginnings.

Unfortunately, it never has been more clear that P.L. 480 is crafted more to help those who give than those who receive. The 1985 changes only reinforce that conclusion.

Summing up: a dirt poor future

The food and farm legislation of 1985 took several steps forward and several back. An encouraging note is that some items on the progressive agenda were for the first time given serious consideration; other positive proposals actually emerged as law. The political struggle over the farm bill was intense, lengthy and exhausting. It became difficult to count the many groups that prepared farm-policy recommendations or agendas leading up to consideration of the bill in 1985. All farm-state Members of Congress were wary of constituent unrest, and Republican Senators up for re-election in 1986 were particularly concerned.

But with the process completed, most of the problems remained unsolved. And overshadowing all federal activity in agriculture and foreign assistance is a grim legislative reaper that may turn out to be far more significant than any farm bill. This is the Gramm-Rudman-Hollings balanced-budget amendment, signed into law on December 12, 1985. Perhaps one of the worst pieces of legislation ever enacted by the Congress, this bill has the potential to decimate most domestic programs of the federal government. Gramm-Rudman grew out of Congressional desperation over the huge federal deficits that have accumulated since 1981. It requires eliminating the $200-plus billion federal budget deficit over a five-year period, which, in the absence of a tax hike, means massive reductions in domestic and military spending. This bill avoids the uncomfortable truth: big deficits are the result of the big tax cuts and big defense build-up begun in 1981. Disastrous cuts in agricultural and other domestic programs can be avoided only through tax increases and defense cuts. Walter Mondale was right, when he said during the 1984 Presidential campaign that a tax hike is essential. Such a hike could and should come through elimination of tax loopholes and subsidies which now cost the Treasury over $400 billion a year.

One of the few bits of silver lining in the Gramm-Rudman cloud is that, along with Social Security and a few other programs, major food assistance spending on the domestic side – food stamps, child nutrition and WIC – is exempt from the legislation's automatic-cuts provision (which feature of the law, as of this writing, has been declared unconstitutional by a lower federal court and is on appeal to the U.S. Supreme Court). But in any case these budget functions are not exempt from cuts during the regular budget process. Other food and farm programs, from soil conservation to Farmers Home Administration loans to foreign assistance, face potentially devastating Gramm-Rudman reductions through 1991. Many of these programs need reform. Many need to be placed on a budgetary diet. But they do not need anorexia or death.

In government and politics, semantics are often of great importance. One spectator sport with words is to observe how food and farm legislative titles have changed over the years. Consider the last few quadrennial farm bills. Once these laws were strictly agricultural, and that was reflected in their titles – for example, the Agricultural Adjustment Act of 1933 and the Agricultural Act of 1949. Then consumer issues were brought into play, first with the Agriculture and Consumer Protection Act of 1973. And now we have 'food security,' with the Food Security Act of 1985. But is there really security? Attempts to cut loose the agricultural sector from stabilizing programs may provide some intellectual security for free market ideologues, but they will do little to secure the farmer. Ultimately they may prove harsh for the consumer as well, as the inflationary experience of the mid-1970s should clearly demonstrate.

At the outset of this chapter, it was observed that few of the reforms put forward in this book or by other progressive critics of food policy were adopted in the major legislation of 1985. There were some clear victories, but much remains to be done. Some reforms will never be accepted, and others will come very slowly. But that does not mean that the long-term effort for change should be abandoned. Far too much is at stake.

There appears to be no approaching light at the end of the tunnel for problems in the food system. There may instead be a false light there, the light of an oncoming crash.

Notes

1 Introduction

1 John E. Lee, 'Food and Agricultural Policy: A Suggested Approach,' *Agricultural-Food Policy Review: Perspectives for the 1980s*, USDA, Economics and Statistics Service, April 1981, p. 140.
2 *Ibid.*, pp. 141-4.

2 Land and food

1 U.S. Department of Agriculture, *A Time to Choose: Summary Report on the Structure of Agriculture*, January 1981, p. xi.
2 George W. Coffman, 'Entry and Exit: Barriers and Incentives,' in *Structure Issues of American Agriculture*, USDA, ESCS, Ag. Econ. Rept. 438, November 1979, p. 116.
3 David H. Harrington *et al.*, *U.S. Farming in the Early 1980s: Production and Financial Structure*, USDA, ERS, Ag. Econ. Rept. 504, September 1983, p. 26.
4 Roy Van Arsdall and Kenneth Nelson, *Characteristics of Farmer Cattle Feeding*, USDA, 1983.
5 Harrington *et al.*, *U.S. Farming in the Early 1980s*, p. 8.
6 *Ibid.*, p. 9.
7 Thomas A. Miller, Gordon E. Rodewald and Robert G. McElroy, *Economies of Size in U.S. Field Crop Farming*, USDA, ESCS, Ag. Econ. Rept. 472, July 1981, p. iii.
8 William Lin, George Coffman and J.B. Penn, *U.S. Farm Numbers, Sizes, and Related Structural Dimensions: Projections to Year 2000*, USDA, ESCS, Tech. Bull. 1625, July 1980.
9 William Lin, James Johnson and Linda Calvin, *Farm Commodity Programs: Who Participates and Who Benefits?*, USDA, ERS, Ag. Econ. Rept. 474, September 1981.

10 U.S. Civil Rights Commission, *The Decline of Black Farming in America*, 1982, p. 5.
11 *Ibid.*, p. 8.
12 USDA, *A Time to Choose*, p. 113.
13 'FY 83 LR Lending: A Mixed Performance,' *Small Farm Advocate*, Fall 1983, p. 6.
14 Dean Hughes *et al.*, *National Agricultural Credit Study: Financing the Farm Sector in the 1980s*, USDA, ESS Staff Report AGESS 810413, April 1981.
15 USDA, *A Time to Choose*, p. 117.
16 Ward Sinclair, 'It's Quittin' Time for Costly, Controversial PIK Farm Program,' *Washington Post*, January 8, 1984.
17 For an analysis, see Ward Sinclair, 'Carter's Granary Saving Reagan,' *Washington Post*, August 28, 1983.
18 William Lin *et al.*, *Farm Commodity Programs: Who Participates and Who Benefits?*, USDA, September 1981.
19 U.S. Department of Commerce, Bureau of the Census, *Money Income of Households, Families, and Persons in the United States: 1981*, Current Population Reports, Series P-60, No. 137, March 1983, pp. 177, 181.
20 USDA, *A Time to Choose*, p. 133.
21 *Ibid.*
22 D. Lillesand, L. Kravitz and J. McClelland, 'An Estimate of the Number of Migrant and Seasonal Farmworkers in the U.S. and Puerto Rico,' Washington, D.C., Legal Services Corporation, 1977.
23 *Hearing on the Migrant and Seasonal Agricultural Worker Protection Act*, U.S. House of Representatives, Committee on Education and Labor, Subcommittee on Labor Standards, September 14, 1982, pp. 68-9.
24 U.S. Department of Labor, Bureau of Labor Statistics, *Occupational Injuries and Illnesses in the United States by Industry*, annual.
25 Agricultural Employment Work Group, *Agricultural Labor in 1980: A Survey with Recommendations*, Center for the Study of Human Resources, University of Texas at Austin, December 1980.
26 Charles Davenport, Michael D. Boehlje and David B.H. Martin, *The Effects of Tax Policy on American Agriculture*, USDA, ERS, Ag. Econ. Rpt. 480, February 1982.
27 Quoted in Joe Belden, 'Who's Farming the Tax Laws?' *People and Taxes*, October 1983.
28 Interfaith Action for Economic Justice, *Tax Breaks: Writing Off the Family Farm*, September 1983, p. 4.
29 *Ibid.*, p. 5.
30 USDA, *A Time to Choose*, p. 148 (italics in original).
31 *Ibid.*, p. 64.
32 Willard F. Mueller, 'The Farm Conglomerates,' in Don F. Hadwiger

and Ross B. Talbot (eds.), *Proceedings of the Academy of Political Science: Food Policy and Farm Programs*, Vol. 34, No. 3, 1982.

33 *Ibid.*, pp. 60-1.

34 *Ibid.*

35 USDA, *Agricultural Statistics 1982*, p. 486. Washington, D.C., U.S. Government Printing Office, p. 486.

3 Fire in the Earth

1 Office of Technology Assessment, *Impacts of Technology on U.S. Cropland and Rangeland Productivity*, U.S. Congress, August 1982.

2 National Agricultural Lands Study, *Soil Degradation: Effects on Agricultural Productivity*, Interim Report No. 4, November 1980, p. 30.

3 U.S. General Accounting Office, *To Protect Tomorrow's Food Supply, Soil Conservation Needs Priority Attention*, CED-77-30, 1977.

4 OTA, *Impacts of Technology*, p. 173.

5 *Ibid.*, pp. 174-5.

6 Many of these recommendations are taken from the OTA report cited above and from the excellent work of the American Farmland Trust (AFT). See the testimony of AFT's Robert J. Gray before the House Agriculture Subcommittee on Conservation, Credit and Rural Development, September 20, 1983.

7 U.S. Geological Survey, *Estimated Use of Water in the United States in 1980*, Circular 1001, 1982.

8 David Pimentel *et al.*, 'Land Degradation: Effects on Food and Energy Resources,' *Science*, October 8, 1976, p. 153.

9 USDA, *Agricultural Statistics 1979*, Washington, D.C., U.S. Government Printing Office, p. 421.

10 Kenneth B. Young and Jerry M. Coomer, *Effects of Natural Gas Price Increases on Texas High Plains Irrigation, 1976-2025*, USDA, ERS, Ag. Econ. Rept. 448, February 1980.

11 OTA, *Impacts of Technology*, p. 46.

12 *Ibid.*, p. 55.

13 Helen Ingram, 'Water Rights in the Western States,' in Don F. Hadwiger and Ross B. Talbot (eds.), *Proceedings of the Academy of Political Science: Food Policy and Farm Programs*, Vol. 34, No. 3, 1982.

14 National Agricultural Lands Study, *Final Report*, Washington, D.C., 1981, p. 4.

15 Robert C. Ottee, *Farming in the City's Shadow*, USDA, ESCS, Ag. Econ. Rept. 250, February 1974, and NALS, *Final Report*, p. 22.

16 John C. Keene *et al.*, *Untaxing Open Space: An Assessment of the Effectiveness of Differential Assessment of Farms and Open Space*, Council on Environmental Quality, April 1976.

17 NALS, *Final Report*, p. 59.

18 W. Wendell Fletcher and Charles E. Little, *The American Cropland Crisis*, Bethesda, Md., American Land Forum, 1982, p. 157.

19 Cornucopia Project, *Empty Breadbasket: The Coming Threat to America's Food Supply*, Emmaus, Penn., Cornucopia Project, 1981, p. 46.
20 *Ibid.*, p. 50.
21 USDA, *Agricultural Statistics 1982*, p. 466.
22 Gordon Sloggett, *Energy and U.S. Agriculture: Irrigation Pumping, 1974-1977*, USDA, ESCS, Ag. Econ. Rept. 436, September 1979, pp. 8-9.
23 Cornucopia Project, *Empty Breadbasket*, p. 28.
24 David Pimentel *et al.*, 'Food Production and the Energy Crisis,' *Science*, November 2, 1973, p. 444.
25 *Ibid.*, p. 448.
26 William Lockeretz *et al.*, *Organic and Conventional Crop Production in the Corn Belt: A Comparison of Economic Performance and Energy Use for Selected Farms*, St. Louis, Washington University Center for the Biology of Natural Systems, 1976.
27 USDA, *Report and Recommendations on Organic Farming*, July 1980.
28 National Academy of Sciences, *Genetic Vulnerability of Major Crops*, Washington, D.C., 1972.
29 Cornucopia Project, *Empty Breadbasket*, pp. 37-8.
30 Jack R. Harlan, 'Crop Monoculture and the Future of American Agriculture,' in Sandra S. Batie and Robert G. Healy (eds.), *The Future of American Agriculture as a Strategic Resource*, Washington, Conservation Foundation, 1980, p. 232.
31 USDA, *Agricultural Statistics 1982*, p. 437.
32 *Ibid.*, p. 436.
33 Cornucopia Project, *Empty Breadbasket*, pp. 50, 56.
34 *Ibid*, pp. 56-7.
35 Leon F. Burmeister, 'Cancer Mortality in Iowa Farmers, 1971–1978,' *Journal of the National Cancer Institute*, March 1981.
36 U.S. Department of State and Council on Environmental Quality, *The Global 2000 Report to the President: Entering the Twenty-first Century*, Vol. 2, 1980, p. 100.
37 Cornucopia Project, *Empty Breadbasket*, pp. 50, 55.
38 Department of State and CEQ, *Global 2000 Report*, Vol. 1, p. 35.

4 Glut of hunger

1 USDA Agricultural Research Service, Consumer and Food Economics Research Divisions, *Family Food Plans Revised 1964*, October 1969, p. 3.
2 Rudolf Penner, testimony to the Subcommittee on Oversight and the Subcommittee on Public Assistance and Unemployment Compensa-

tion, Committee on Ways and Means, U.S. House of Representatives, October 18, 1983.

3 U.S. Department of Commerce, Bureau of the Census, *Estimates of Poverty, Including the Value of Noncash Benefits, 1979-1982*, Technical paper 51, February 1984.

4 *Ibid.*

5 Memo on Poverty Statistics, dated July 31, 1984, from Gary Bass, Executive Director, OMB Watch, Washington, D.C.

6 U.S. House of Representatives, Committee on Ways and Means, *Background Material and Data on Programs Within the Jurisdiction of the Committee on Ways and Means*, Committee Print 98-22, February 21, 1984.

7 U.S. House of Representatives, Committee on Ways and Means, *Background on Poverty*, Committee Print 98-15, October 17, 1983, p. 82.

8 U.S. Congress, Congressional Budget Office, *Major Legislative Changes in Human Services Programs Since January 1981*, August 1983.

9 U.S. Department of Labor, Bureau of Labor Statistics, *The Employment Situation*, November 1983.

10 Robert Greenstein, Center on Budget and Policy Priorities, Washington, D.C., testimony before the President's Taskforce on Food Assistance, November 16, 1983.

11 U.S. Congress, Congressional Budget Office, *op. cit.*

12 U.S. Department of Agriculture, *Characteristics of Food Stamp Households, 1981*, Washington, D.C., July 1982.

13 U.S. Congress, Congressional Budget Office, *op. cit.*

14 Center on Budget and Policy Priorities, *Yes, Mr. Meese, There IS Hunger in America*, Washington, D.C., December 1983.

15 U.S. Congress, Congressional Budget Office, *op. cit.*

16 Center on Budget and Policy Priorities, *op. cit.*

17 Food Research and Action Center, *The Impact of Child Nutrition Budget Cuts*, Washington D.C., 1982.

18 U.S. Conference of Mayors, *Human Services in FY 1982*, Washington, D.C., November 1982.

19 U.S. Conference of Mayors, *Hunger in American Cities*, Washington, D.C., June 1983.

20 Social and Scientific Systems, Inc., *A Report on Nine Case Studies of Emergency Food Assistance Programs*, submitted to the U.S. Department of Agriculture, Washington, D.C., May 1983.

21 U.S. General Accounting Office, *Public and Private Efforts to Feed America's Poor*, Washington, D.C., June 23, 1983, p. 7.

22 Citizens' Commission on Hunger in New England, *American Hunger Crisis*, Harvard School of Public Health, Boston, 1984, pp. 14-16.

23 Harris Survey, February 2, 1984, ISSN 0273-1037.

24 All statistics are from U.S. Department of Agriculture, *Character-istics of Food Stamp Households: August 1982*, July 1984.

25 *Report of the President's Task Force on Food Assistance*, Washington, D.C., January 1984, p. 38.

26 U.S. Department of Agriculture, Consumer Nutrition Center, *Food Consumption and Dietary Levels of Low Income Households, November, 1977, Nationwide Food Consumption Survey, 1977-78, Preliminary Report No. 8,* Washington, D.C., Government Printing Office, 1981.

27 Food Research and Action Center, *Still Hungry: A Survey of People in Need of Emergency Food*, Washington, D.C., November 1983, p. 1.

28 Maryland Food Committee, *Report to the President's Task Force on Food Assistance*, Baltimore, December 1983.

29 *Food Stamp and Commodity Distribution Amendments of 1981*, Report of the Committee on Agriculture, Nutrition, and Forestry, United States Senate, Together with Additional Views to Accompany S1007, June 2, 1981, Washington, D.C., U.S. Government Printing Office, p. 24.

30 Participation data are taken from the *Report of the President's Task Force on Food Assistance*, January 1984.

31 Richard Coe, 'A Longitudinal Analysis of Non Participation in the Food Stamp Program by Eligible Households.' Washington, D.C., U.S. Department of Health and Human Services, January 31, 1985.

32 Betty Peterkin and Mary Hama, 'Food Shopping Skills of the Rich and the Poor,' *Family Economics Review*, No. 3, July 1983.

33 The Recommended Dietary Allowances (RDA) are recommendations for the average daily amounts of nutrients that population groups should consume over a period of time. The Food and Nutrition Board, under whose auspices the RDA is developed, states: 'In assessing dietary surveys of populations, if the amounts of nutrients consumed fall below the RDA for a particular age/sex group, some individuals can be assumed to be at nutritional risk. When the proportion of individuals with such low intakes is extensive, the risk of deficiency in the population is increased.' They also state: 'it is clear that the more habitual intake falls below the RDA and the longer the low intake continues, the greater is the risk of deficiency.' (Committee on Dietary Allowances, Food and Nutrition Board, *Recommended Dietary Allowances, Ninth Revised Edition, 1980*, Washington, D.C., National Academy of Sciences, 1980.)

Recommended *Dietary* Allowances, the basis for all the food programs and nutritional status surveys, should not be confused with the U.S. Recommended *Daily* Allowances. The latter were developed by the Food and Drug Administration as legal standards for labeling the nutritional content of food, and to provide consumers with accurate and reliable information; they were developed on the basis of the 1968 Recommended Dietary Allowances.

34 Betty Peterkin, Richard L. Kerr and Mary Hama, 'Nutritional Adequacies of Diets of Low Income Households,' *Journal of Nutrition Education*, Vol. 14, No. 3, 1982, p. 102.

35 *Ibid.*

36 Food Research and Action Center. *Still Hungry.*

37 U.S. General Accounting Office, *WIC Evaluations Produce Some Favorable Results But No Conclusive Evidence on the Effects Expected for the Special Supplemental Food Program for Women, Infants and Children*, January 30, 1984.

38 *Report of the President's Task Force on Food Assistance*, January 1984.

39 U.S. Department of Agriculture, *The National School Lunch Program and Diets of Participants from Low-Income Households*, 1981.

40 J.B. Wellish *et al.*, *The National Evaluation of School Nutrition Programs: Final Report*, Santa Monica, Cal., System Development Corporation, April 1983.

41 J.S. Akin *et al.*, 'Nutritional Effect of School Lunch and School Breakfast,' presentation at the Agricultural Outlook Conference, December 1982, Washington, D.C.

42 *Ibid.*

43 Maureen Staggenborg, *Family Day Care Survey and Position Paper*, State of Connecticut Department of Education, Hartford, Conn., April 1983.

44 Abt Associates, *Evaluation of the Child Care Food Program*, Cambridge, Mass., February 1983, p. 3.

45 Public Law 92-258, Section 701.

46 Public Law 89-73, Section 305 (a) (2) (E) and Section 306 (a) (5) (A).

47 CFR, Title 45, 1321.3.

48 U.S. Department of Health and Human Services, Administration on Aging, *FY 1983 National Summary of Program Performance*, 1984.

49 *Ibid.*

50 U.S. Department of Commerce, Bureau of the Census, *Money Income and Poverty Status of Families and Persons in the U.S.: 1982*, Series P-60, No. 124, March 1984, p. 21.

51 Kirschner Associates Inc., *An Evaluation of the Nutrition Services for the Elderly*, Vol. II, Albuquerque, N.M., 1983, pp. VII-8 and VIII-7.

52 U.S. Department of Commerce, Bureau of the Census, *America in Transition: An Aging Society*, Series P-23, No. 128, September 1983, p. 1.

53 U.S. Department of Agriculture, *Food Consumption of Households in the United States: Report No. 1*, Washington, D.C., U.S.

Government Printing Office, Spring 1965.

54 *Poverty, Hunger and Federal Food Programs: Background Information*, Subcommittee on Employment, Manpower and Poverty, Committee on Labor and Public Welfare, U.S. Senate, July 1967.

55 USDA, Consumer Nutrition Center, *Food Consumption and Dietary Levels of Low Income Households*, 1981.

56 *Final Report*, Select Committee on Nutrition and Human Needs, U.S. Senate, December 1977.

5 *World hunger, world markets*

1 Quoted in *Overcoming World Hunger: The Challenge Ahead*, Report of the Presidential Commission on World Hunger, March 1980, p. 16, Washington, D.C., U.S. Government Printing Office.

2 *The United States and World Development – Agenda 1980*, by John W. Sewell and the staff of the Overseas Development Council, New York, Praeger, 1980, p. 60.

3 Richard Gilmore, *A Poor Harvest*, New York, Longman, 1982, p. 20.

4 James Wessel with Mort Hantman, *Trading the Future*, San Francisco, Institute for Food and Development Policy, 1983, p. 3.

5 *Ibid.*, p. 109 (italics in original).

6 Gilmore, *op. cit.*, p. 14.

7 Sewell, *op. cit.* p. 60.

8 Joint Hearing, Committee on Agriculture and Committee on Foreign Affairs, House of Representatives, 98th Congress, April 7, 1983, p. 94.

9 *Overcoming World Hunger*, p. 19.

10 *Dirty Grain*, pamphlet issued by the Center for Development Policy, Washington, D.C., n.d. [1978].

11 *Ibid.*

12 Thomas R. Graham, 'The Global Trade: War and Peace,' *Foreign Policy*, No. 50, Spring 1983, p. 130.

13 *Ibid.*, pp. 124-37.

14 Gilmore, *op. cit.*, p. 194.

15 *Ibid.*, p. 197.

16 Tony Jackson, *Against the Grain: The Dilemma of Project Food Aid*, Oxford, Oxfam, 1982.

17 *Washington Post*, September 25, 1983.

18 *World Hunger: Causes and Remedies*, Washington, D.C., Transnational Institute, 1974, p. 118.

19 Figures from U.S. Agency for International Development, *World Development Letter*, Vol. 3, No. 5, March 3, 1980.

20 Independent Commission on International Development Issues,

North-South: A Program for Survival, Cambridge, Mass. MIT Press, 1983, p. 14.
21 *Overcoming World Hunger*, p. 140.
22 *Ibid.*, p. 141.
23 Institute for Food and Development Policy, *The Aid Debate*, Working Paper No. 1, San Francisco, 1979, p. 6.
24 Wessel, *op. cit.*, p. 155.
25 *Multinational Monitor*, May 1982, p. 17.
26 *Food Monitor*, December 1977, p. 11.
27 U.S. General Accounting Office, Report to Congress, *World Hunger and Malnutrition Continue: Slow Progress in Carrying Out World Food Conference Objectives*, January 11, 1980, p. 5.
28 Michael Perelman, *Farming for Profit in a Hungry World*, New York, Allanheld, Osmun & Co., 1977.
29 Overseas Development Council and Charles F. Kettering Foundation, *Interdependent*, July/August, 1981.
30 *Overcoming World Hunger*, pp. 140 ff.
31 Joint Hearing, Committee on Agriculture and Committee on Foreign Affairs, House of Representatives, 98th Congress, April 7, 1983, p. 52.
32 *World Hunger and Malnutrition Continue*, p. 6.
33 *Overcoming World Hunger*, p. 79.
34 Richard J. Barnet, *The Lean Years: Politics in the Age of Scarcity*, New York, Simon and Schuster, 1980, p. 165.
35 Gilmore, *op.cit.*, p. 240.
36 *World Hunger and Malnutrition Continue*, p. 12.
37 *Food Policy Notes*, March 23, 1984, Note #84-12, p. 3, Washington, D.C., Interfaith Action for Economic Justice.
38 *North–South: A Program for Survival*, p. 117.
39 *World Hunger and Malnutrition Continue*, p. 15.
40 Guy Gran, *Development by People – Citizen Construction of a Just World*, New York, Praeger, 1983.

6 Conclusions

1 Quoted in Marj Charlier, 'Rural Crisis May Hurt Rest of the Economy, Many Experts Believe,' *Wall Street Journal*, December 24, 1985.
2 Ward Sinclair, 'The World Doesn't Need Our Farmers,' *Washington Post*, December 29, 1985.
3 Dennis Avery, 'U.S. Farm Dilemma: The Global Bad News Is Wrong,' *Science*, October 25, 1985.

Select bibliography

General

Belden, Joe, *et al.* (eds.), *New Directions in Farm, Land and Food Policy: A Time for State and Local Action*, Washington: Conference on Alternative State and Local Policies, 1979.

Belden, Joe, and Gregg Forte, *Toward a National Food Policy*, Washington: Exploratory Project for Economic Alternatives, 1976.

Benedict, Murray R., *Farm Policies of the United States, 1790-1950*, New York: Twentieth Century Fund, 1953.

Buttel, Frederick, and Howard Newby (eds.), *The Rural Sociology of the Advanced Societies*, Montclair, N.J.: Allanheld, Osmun, 1980.

Goodwyn, Lawrence, *Democratic Promise*, New York: Oxford University Press, 1976.

Hadwiger, Don, and William Browne, *The New Politics of Food*, Lexington, Mass.: Lexington Books, 1978.

Hadwiger, Don, and Ross Talbot (eds.), *Food Policy and Farm Programs*, Academy of Political Science (Vol. 34, No. 3), 1982.

Kahn, E.J., *The Staffs of Life*, Boston: Little, Brown, 1984.

Lerza, Catherine, and Michael Jacobson, *Food for People, Not For Profit*, New York: Ballantine, 1975.

McGovern, George (ed.), *Agricultural Thought in the Twentieth Century*, Indianapolis: Bobbs-Merrill, 1967.

National Advisory Commission on Rural Poverty, *The People Left Behind*, 1967.

Rodefeld, Richard, *et al.* (eds.), *Change in Rural America*, St. Louis: C.V. Mosby, 1978.

U.S. Department of Agriculture, *1985 Factbook of US Agriculture*, November 1984.

Wilcox, Walter W., *et al.*, *Economics of American Agriculture*, Englewood Cliffs, N.J.: Prentice-Hall, 1974.

Working Group on Food and Farm Policy, *Beyond Crisis: Farm and Food Policy for Tomorrow*, December 1984.

183

Agriculture and the family farm

Cochrane, Willard, *The Development of American Agriculture*, Minneapolis: University of Minnesota Press, 1979.

Cochrane, Willard, and Mary Ryan, *American Farm Policy: 1948–1973*, Minneapolis: University of Minnesota Press, 1976.

Goldschmidt, Walter, *As You Sow*, Montclair, N.J.: Allanheld, Osmun, 1978.

Hightower, Jim, and Susan DeMarco, *Hard Tomatoes, Hard Times*, Cambridge, Mass.: Schenkman, 1972.

Kramer, Mark, *Three Farms*, Boston: Little, Brown, 1980.

Paarlberg, Don, *Farm and Food Policy*, Lincoln: University of Nebraska Press, 1980.

Sachs, Carolyn, *The Invisible Farmers: Women in Agricultural Production*, Totowa, N.J.: Rowman & Allanheld, 1983.

U.S. Commission on Civil Rights, *The Decline of Black Farming in America*, 1982.

U.S. Congress, Joint Economic Committee, *Toward the Next Generation of Farm Policy* (Hearings), May/June 1983.

U.S. Congressional Budget Office, *Public Policy and the Changing Structure of American Agriculture*, 1978.

U.S. Department of Agriculture, *A Time to Choose: Summary Report on the Structure of Agriculture*, January 1981.

U.S. Department of Agriculture, Economic Research Service, *Agricultural-Food Policy Review*, Ag. Econ. Rpt. 530, July 1985.

U.S. Department of Agriculture, Economics, Statistics and Cooperatives Service, *Structure Issues of American Agriculture*, Ag. Econ. Rpt. 438, November 1979.

U.S. General Accounting Office, *Changing Character and Structure of American Agriculture*, 1978.

U.S. Senate, Committee on Agriculture, Nutrition and Forestry, *Farm Structure* (Committee Print), April 1980.

Consumer issues

Gussow, Joan, *The Feeding Web*, Palo Alto, Calif.: Bull, 1978.

Hall, Ross, *Food for Nought*, New York: Vintage, 1976.

Hightower, Jim, *Eat Your Heart Out*, New York: Crown, 1975.

Jacobson, Michael, *Eater's Digest*, New York: Doubleday, 1970.

Kotz, Nick, *Let Them Eat Promises*, New York: Doubleday, 1971.

Lipsky, Michael, and Marc Thibodeau, *Food in the Warehouses, Hunger in the Streets*, Massachusetts Institute of Technology, July 1985.

Turner, Jim, *The Chemical Feast*, New York: Grossman, 1972.

Wellford, Harrison, *Sowing the Wind*, New York: Grossman, 1972.

Environment, resources, technology

American Farmland Trust, *Soil Conservation in America*, Washington: American Farmland Trust, 1984.
Barnet, Richard, *The Lean Years*, New York: Simon & Schuster, 1980.
Berry, Wendell, *The Unsettling of America*, New York: Avon, 1978.
Blobaum, Roger, *The Loss of Agricultural Land*, Washington: Citizens Advisory Commission on Environmental Quality, 1974.
Brown, Lester, *Building a Sustainable Society*, New York: Norton, 1982.
Brown, Lester, *et al.*, *State of the World 1984*, New York: Norton, 1984
Brown, Lester, *et al.*, *State of the World 1985*, New York: Norton, 1985.
Cornucopia Project, *Empty Breadbasket*, Emmaus, Pa.: Rodale, 1981.
Doyle, Jack, *Altered Harvest*, New York: Viking, 1985.
Eckholm, Erik, *Losing Ground*, New York: Norton, 1976.
Merrill, Richard, *Radical Agriculture*, New York: Harper & Row, 1976.
National Agricultural Land Study, *Final Report*, 1981.
Perelman, Michael, *Farming for Profit in a Hungry World*, Montclair, N.J.: Allanheld & Osmun, 1978.
Sampson, Neil, *Farmland or Wasteland?*, Emmaus, Pa.: Rodale, 1981.
U.S. Department of State and Council on Environmental Quality, *The Global 2000 Report to the President*, 1980.
U.S. Office of Technology Assessment, *Impacts of Technology on U.S. Cropland and Rangeland Productivity*, 1982.

International development and world hunger

Brandt, Willy, *et al.*, *North-South: A Program for Survival*, Cambridge, Mass.: MIT Press, 1980.
Brown, Lester, with Erik Eckholm, *By Bread Alone*, New York: Praeger, 1974.
de Castro, Josue, *The Geopolitics of Hunger*, New York: Monthly Review, 1977.
George, Susan, *Feeding the Few*, Washington: Institute for Policy Studies, 1981.
George, Susan, *How the Other Half Dies*, Montclair, N.J.: Allanheld & Osmun, 1977.
Gilmore, Richard, *A Poor Harvest*, New York: Longman, 1982.
Gran, Guy, *Development by People*, New York: Praeger, 1983.
Jackson, Tony, *Against the Grain*, Oxford: Oxfam, 1982.
Lappé, Frances, *Diet for a Small Planet*, New York: Ballantine, 1983.
Lappé, Frances, *et al.*, *Food First*, New York: Ballantine, 1977.
Morgan, Dan, *Merchants of Grain*, New York: Viking, 1979.
Presidential Commission on World Hunger, *Overcoming World Hunger: The Challenge Ahead*, March 1980.
U.S. Department of Agriculture, Economic Research Service, *World Food Needs and Availability, 1985*, July 1985.

Index